BUSY LIVES & RESTLESS SOULS

Busy Lives & Restless Souls

How Prayer Can Help You
Find the Missing Peace in
Your Life

BECKY ELDREDGE

LOYOLA PRESS.
A JESUIT MINISTRY
Chicago

LOYOLA PRESS.
A JESUIT MINISTRY

3441 N. Ashland Avenue
Chicago, Illinois 60657
(800) 621-1008
www.loyolapress.com

Cover art credit: Illustrations: dashk/iStock/Getty Images., Background texture: kokoroyuki/iStock/Thinkstock

ISBN-13: 978-0-8294-4495-7
ISBN-10: 0-8294-4495-5
Library of Congress Control Number: 2016957356

Printed in the United States of America.
19 20 21 22 23 24 25 Versa 10 9 8 7 6 5 4

For Chris

"Rejoice. Let your kindness be known to all.
The Lord is near!"

—Philippians 4:5

Contents

Foreword

One of the reasons the writings of St. Ignatius continue to serve us well five centuries later is that he himself understood that his instructions would need to be adapted for the various situations wherein they would be employed. He was fond of giving a firm directive but then telling the reader that it should be adjusted "in view of the circumstances of places, times and persons." He believed so strongly in this adaptation that at times he makes us laugh. As novice director, I read together with the novices St. Ignatius's rule for the Jesuits, the *Constitutions of the Society of Jesus*. Again and again, this headstrong Basque tells his Jesuits that such and such must be carried out exactly in this particular way, but then adds, "unless it seems prudent to do otherwise." This "always do it this way . . . unless you discern otherwise" makes us chuckle from time to time. An example of this from his Spiritual Exercises is in his Fourth Annotation wherein Ignatius explains that the full retreat is divided into four weeks. Then he says, "It is not to be understood that each week has, of necessity, seven or eight days. For, as it happens that in the first week some are slower to find what they seek . . . it is necessary sometimes to shorten the week, and at other times lengthen it." Well enough, but then Ignatius tries but fails to lay down a stricter rule: "However, the Exercises will be finished in thirty days . . . a little more or less."

As humorous as it may sound at times, it is this very characteristic of St. Ignatius that has made his work as fruitful today as in the sixteenth century. Ignatius had the foresight to know that the interior life must be adapted to fit the circumstances of the exterior life. To be sure, the God we encounter in different places and in different ages "is the same yesterday, today and forever," but how we experience that same God is affected by the exterior circumstances of life. The Ignatian teachings of spiritual desolation and consolation hold as true for a sixteenth-century Basque priest as they do for a twenty-first-century American wife and mother. But the two will experience these truths differently because of the dramatic contrast in their exterior lives. Ignatian spirituality endures through the ages precisely because Ignatius got just right the balance between the unshakeable foundations of our faith and the supple fluidity of its lived expression.

This is why this book is so groundbreaking and important: In her own life, Becky Eldredge has discovered ways of living out the lasting truths of St. Ignatius as she meets the challenges, opportunities, joys, and struggles of a contemporary American wife and mom. For too long, the written explications of Ignatian spirituality have been the exclusive work of Jesuit priests. Finally, we return to Ignatius's great insight about adaptability and allow a fresh new voice from a fresh new perspective to break through.

And what a freshness! A great gift of Ignatian spirituality is the Application of the Senses, the use of our imagination to prayerfully envision ourselves as characters in the biblical stories. Ignatian writers have taught this for centuries. But only now, the Ignatian world gets to read how a mom prayerfully experiences Mary holding the baby Jesus in her arms. Only now do we reflect on the "young love" of our relationship with God through the life experience of a young American couple, laboriously and yet endearingly negotiating the way this new family will wash its Cajun cast-iron skillet.

Perhaps what I as a Jesuit priest and spiritual writer appreciate most is the overarching thesis of Eldredge's work, strikingly articulated near the end of the book:

> People question me all the time because of my age at pursuing a life of prayer during the season of life I am in. They imply that my relationship with God should somehow be delayed to a later season, when my kids are no longer in my house or when my professional career is further along. I cannot count the number of times people have, to my face, questioned the ministry work I do, causing immense doubt in me. Every time, though, I bring this doubt to God in prayer, and God affirms my call to both be in relationship with God and to do the work I do.
>
> So this is why I am here, now, writing this book. Because I hope that you hear a different message from me than I heard at times. The time for prayer is now. I do not care what is going on in your life—if you are raising kids or are an empty nester. I don't care if you are working eighteen hours a day seven days a week or are faced with hours of loneliness a day. It doesn't matter if you are young or old, single or married, religious or ordained. The time for prayer is now.

It was not that hard for me to rise before sunrise this morning, grab a cup of strong Louisiana coffee, and begin my Ignatian meditation in my quiet little bedroom in a house full of priests, brothers, and seminarians. I have no experience, however, of being awoken by pajama-wearing, sweet, squealing little kids jumping in my bed. As an administrator, I have lots of experience poring over profit-and-loss sheets, but I don't know what it's like—in the midst of changing diapers and straightening toy rooms—to worry about how my family will make ends meet in a new city and in a depressed economy. Because I have no such experience, I perhaps lend too much credence to the naysayers who claim, "Sure, a regular, sustained prayer life is possible for a celibate priest, but not for a struggling young mom." It is not for me to dispute such a claim. It takes a young, Ignatian wife, mom, and professional woman to stand strong and tell the world that such a person exists.

And not only exists, but thrives.

—Mark E. Thibodeaux, SJ

Introduction

One Friday night in March 2011, I stepped outside a chapel in Athens, Georgia, into the cool evening air during a period of silent prayer at a weekend retreat. It was a retreat for those in their twenties and thirties, based on the spirituality of St. Ignatius.

As the doors of the chapel closed behind me, I caught a glimpse of thirty of my peers sitting in total silence and prayer in the chapel. The silence followed me as I took a few deep breaths outside. There, I noticed the world alive around me. Across our church's parking lot, a young woman, along with her family and friends, celebrated her quinceañera in our main building. The pounding music and laughter of the people drifted across the church parking lot as the doors to the main building opened and closed. I breathed in the joy of the moment.

In the distance, I heard the crack of a baseball bat and the cheering of fans at the University of Georgia baseball game. I smiled at the cheers, knowing something good had just happened in the game. I breathed in the excitement of our community.

Then I looked up because of the sound of approaching helicopters. They were flying low and moving quickly, their lights scanning the area. I knew they were looking for a young man who had shot and killed a police officer in our community days earlier. I breathed in the sadness of their search.

All at once, I found myself overcome with the understanding that God was in all of these moments at the same time: God speaking to each man and woman in silent prayer in the chapel; God celebrating with those at the party; God savoring the community's enjoyment of the baseball game; and God in the search for that young man, comforting the family and friends of the fallen police officer, comforting the family of the man on the run, and offering wisdom in the decisions made by the man and by the officers who sought him.

I was overwhelmed with clarity that night of God in all things and God active in each moment of our lives. Everything seemed holy.

✝

That night was not unique in its holding a multitude of events that carried both joy and pain. It was not unique in the reality of God present in each aspect of it. It was unique because within the silence of my heart I *saw* God in each moment. Years of grounding myself in Ignatian spirituality—both the practice and teaching of it—had culminated in a clarity of understanding the real truth of St. Ignatius's teaching: that God is in all things and that everything in life is holy.

Now, I am not a monk. I did not take the vows of holy orders. I am not called to the religious life. I am a woman in her midthirties who offers retreats and spiritual direction to people of all ages and in all stages of life and who lives this reality herself. The walls of my home echo with the voices of children and conversations with my husband. My prayer life happens within the realities of raising children, working, and helping support our family. It happens amid carpools and diaper changes, shuttling kids to practices, making meals, and doing laundry. It happens within my marriage and within all the joys and responsibilities of the other relationships in my life. It happens during trying times of transition, change, and loss, and also in moments of joy.

I am a woman who lives a normal life, perhaps not unlike you. But I have found that the wisdom of St. Ignatius, a saint who lived five hundred years ago, offers much for the moments we live right now. He can teach us how to find God in our most mundane minutes and amid our most difficult questions. He can help us name the restlessness in our lives. He can show us how to find God right where we are.

I am someone whose profession it is to walk with others in their faith lives through spiritual direction, writing, retreats, and teaching on prayer. As I seek to do within my ministry work, I aim to equip you through this book with tools of prayer that you can bring into daily life. I will offer prayer tools that are accessible within the busyness and fullness of your life. Together, we will learn how

- prayer helps you see God in all things;
- prayer awakens you to God's love;
- prayer makes you aware of God's light in the darkness;
- prayer roots you within the reality of your experience;
- prayer holds you steady through the hard times;
- prayer calls you outward; and
- prayer brings you the grace of joy.

A Word on St. Ignatius and Ignatian Spirituality

So that you understand my approach in this book, it is important for you to know a bit about St. Ignatius and the spirituality attributed to him that is called Ignatian spirituality. You may be surprised to hear that the legacy St. Ignatius left behind more than five hundred years ago resonates strongly with our experience of the twenty-first century, so I'm going to take a few moments to share with you about this saint and how his approach is still so relevant.

Much of Ignatian spirituality finds its roots in St. Ignatius's recorded experiences of prayer and of his experiences of God. His gift was taking the insights he gleaned from his own prayer life and putting them into words others could understand. His spirituality offers us a way of meeting God and being with God, and his story reminds us that our own faith stories are not all that different from his.

So who was this saint whose legacy lives on today? St. Ignatius was born in Spain and grew up a son in a wealthy family. He was a soldier and a well-known womanizer. In a battle in Pamplona, Spain, he was struck in the leg and severely injured by a cannonball. He endured many procedures in order to fix his leg. After one such procedure, he became so sick that his family feared for his life. After the leg bone healed, it left an "unsightly bump," and because "he was determined to make a way for himself in the world, he could not tolerate such ugliness and thought it marred his appearance."[1] Ignatius, despite recommendations from his family and doctor, underwent another procedure to remove the bump. It was Ignatius's pride and vanity that left him many days recovering in bed with not much to do but read.

Two books were available to him: *The Imitation of Christ* and a book on the lives of the saints. During his hours in bed, Ignatius read these two books and found himself dreaming what his life would be like if he followed the lives of the saints and gave up his career as a soldier. At times, he would pray about following the saints and noticed a great peace fill him that lasted long after prayer. At other times, he would dream of continuing to be a soldier and noticed that this same peace would come briefly but not linger quite as long.

Ignatius began paying attention to how he felt as he pondered which way he wanted to live. One way, the worldly way of ambition

---

1. Joseph Tylenda, *A Pilgrim's Journey: The Autobiography of Ignatius of Loyola* (San Francisco: Ignatius Press, 2001), 42.

and success, brought him peace for a short time but would soon leave him feeling dry and empty. The other way, following in the footsteps of Christ and the saints, left him with a peace that lasted for a long time.

Eventually, Ignatius came to realize that God was inviting him to put down his sword and to live a life of prayer and faith, modeled on the saints. It was this experience of pondering what God asked of him that helped Ignatius flesh out his discernment wisdom—the same discernment wisdom many religious orders and various Christian denominations use today as a way of figuring out God's invitations to us.

Upon full recovery, Ignatius let his family know of his plans to no longer be a soldier. As many of us do when we start taking steps toward a new way of life, he met resistance from his family and friends. Dedicated to following the desires of his heart, Ignatius set out and began living a life modeled on Jesus and the saints. Through his prayer experiences, St. Ignatius crafted the text of the *Spiritual Exercises*, a series of meditations and praying with Scripture that ultimately leads a person into an intimate friendship with Jesus. The wisdom that comes from the *Spiritual Exercises* forms the basis for what is now known as Ignatian spirituality.

St. Ignatius and Me

A lot of books have been written on the life of St. Ignatius, and much could be said about him. But let me tell you in a nutshell why this saint who lived more than five hundred years ago matters to me, an American woman in her thirties who is a wife and mother of three and who, like so many, is trying to use her gifts in her family, her profession, and the world.

St. Ignatius's story and initial call to follow God happened when he was a young adult. His story of conversion occurred when he was in his twenties, and some of his greatest insights into spirituality happened when he was under the age of forty. My conversion, too, started at a young age—I was just sixteen—and I find myself surprised to be writing at length about prayer and spirituality in what is just my fourth decade of life. I draw much strength from St. Ignatius's example because my age in the realm of the work I do as a spiritual director, writer, and retreat facilitator is different from the norm. Ignatius reminds me that God can use us and call us no matter what our age.

Additionally, Ignatius's conversion came unexpectedly and through circumstances right in front of him. His story reminds me that our call to begin a faith journey can come at any point and at any age and that God will work from where we are. This brings a deep peace—to know that God is not done with any of us yet and that God will not stop laboring for us until we are in a dynamic relationship with the divine.

St. Ignatius's story also reminds me that God can use anyone to be part of the work of the kingdom. Why would God pick Ignatius when many more "saintly" people could have been picked to do what he did? How often I ask God that question about myself! Why me, God? And yet we see through St. Ignatius that this question is not God's question. God will use whomever God wills.

Another draw for me is that Ignatian spirituality is more than five hundred years old. In this day and age, when we are often caught up in the latest trend or fleeting fad, I find relief in the credibility of a spirituality that has survived this long and continues to speak to people today. In a time when commitments and longevity are rare, there is a comfort in knowing that this approach to prayer and life with God is not a latest trend but one that has survived and still thrives.

The more I read about St. Ignatius, the more I like him. Many of his characteristics are part of our culture today. His vanity, for instance, was so ridiculous that he had the doctors fix his leg because he thought it didn't look right. He possessed an ambition that rivals our American dream to be successful and wealthy and have it all. Ignatius's thought was, *I can do it better than St. Dominic and St. Francis.* It was this pride and ambition that set him out on his conversion experience in order to emulate and outdo the saints he revered. Like many of us, Ignatius eventually came to realize he could not live a life of faith by powering through on his own but needed God to help him on his journey. As with Ignatius, God is going to call us, despite our pride, our vanity, and our sinfulness, to be part of God's work in the world.

While St. Ignatius lived more than five hundred years ago, my life is deeply touched by the wisdom and practices he offers us in our prayer and life with God. It was his spirituality that was a basis for the education I received from the Sisters of St. Joseph of Medaille in grades K–12. Long before I could name it, I was picking up nuggets of St. Ignatius's wisdom from the environment of my elementary school and high school and the people who taught me in those places. It was his spirituality that formed me in my early years of ministry as a college student and young professional. It was his spirituality that grounded the master's degree in pastoral studies I completed at Loyola University in New Orleans. It was his Spiritual Exercises I completed in my late twenties with the help of a spiritual director. The Jesuit retreat organization I worked with for eight years, Charis Ministries, finds its mission and identity in bringing the gifts of Ignatian spirituality to those in their twenties and thirties. It was this spirituality that formed the basis of my training to become a spiritual director through Spring Hill College, a Jesuit school.

I feel that I am a daughter of Ignatius. At times I joke that I am a "Jesuitte," a woman who lives and breathes the very spirituality that guides the Jesuits, the all-men's religious order Ignatius founded. Ignatian spirituality permeates my life, my marriage, and my motherhood.

It forms the basis of my ministry as a writer, spiritual director, and retreat facilitator.

Through the tools St. Ignatius offers, Ignatian spirituality teaches us how to pray our lives and bring all of our life to God. The prayer tools and concepts of Ignatian spirituality help us live a life of prayer within our daily realities. Because, the truth is, Ignatian prayer is not just about being with God but also about the action that springs forth from our time with God—what St. Ignatius called being a *contemplative in action*. We might not be called to formal religious life, but we can live our faith in the normal activities that fill our days.

In the pages ahead, I hope you understand that the invitation to connect your faith with your daily life is an invitation God urges all of us to accept. All of us are invited to a relationship with God in the middle of our lives. God labors to fill us, complete us, and make us whole. God dreams that every aspect of our lives will be affected and energized by our relationship with God. And the great news is that God always acts first. The example of our entire salvation history is that God initiates and we respond. Our choice is simply this: *Will I respond to this invitation or not?*

I hope your answer is yes! I believe that if you respond to God's invitation, you will come to understand what I, too, have come to know is true—that indeed, everything is holy now.

1

Acknowledging the Restlessness

On senior retreat in high school, I experienced silent prayer for the first time. One of my religion teachers invited us into one hour of silence on a sunny October afternoon in Louisiana. I can close my eyes now and still picture the lake that was the backdrop of that experience. I can remember the gentle way the wind rustled through the trees and blew my hair. I can see the cloudless, bright blue sky, vibrant with the sun's rays. It was a moment in which everything felt holy.

But I was not sure what to *do* with this silent prayer time. The retreat was packed with activities and directives. I felt unsure and anxious about how I was going to survive an hour of silence alone—an extrovert's worst nightmare. How would I last without talking? I was a bit afraid of this freedom I was given to "go enjoy my time with God."

Aimless, I wandered the retreat grounds until I found a spot on a levee overlooking the lake. I gazed at my friends who were scattered around the lake and retreat grounds and who looked just as lost as I felt.

And yet, despite my fears, something stirred from deep within. I felt it knocking, begging to be acknowledged and released. I could not put a name to it, but something felt awakened after a long period of dormancy. In truth, this gnawing sensation had been building for more than a year, but on the levee that day, I grappled with this powerful presence at work in me. I had no words for the hunger that was asking me for more. All I could do was attempt to be still and acknowledge its existence.

I took a deep breath and looked to God above, begging for help with what felt like an insurmountable task: sitting still and being quiet. Slowly, as the deep breaths continued, inner stillness came. I began to notice my surroundings. In that moment, I saw everything as it was—beautiful, holy, God's gift. My heart welled to the point that I thought it would leap out of my chest. I realized that the hunger I felt was my desire for God. For one solid hour, I breathed deeply in the silence and in being with God.

On that day, I touched something powerful: God within me, residing in the inner space that only God and I can access. I understood that holiness lived within me as much as it lived outside me in the beautiful surroundings of the retreat grounds. I could not name then what, with clarity, I can now, eighteen years later, identify as a major point in my faith journey, a moment that changed the trajectory of my life. This telling moment of silence fueled me on a path to return to God, who resided in the silence of my heart. I also realized, in that moment, that my very restlessness was God speaking to my soul.

A Restlessness We Need

The need for silence and stillness is a common theme of our culture right now. In my city's newspaper and in various magazines I read articles about the impact of the overconnectedness we experience through technology. I read about the impact of overscheduling our children's lives as well as our own. On the sidelines of my children's soccer games, at birthday parties, and at school functions, my peers and I discuss how busy we are, how hectic our day-to-day lives are, and how there never seems to be time to slow down and catch our breath. In these conversations, I hear a longing for something else, a yearning for another way, a hunger for something deeper.

I will never forget a conversation with a man at one of my children's activities. Upon hearing that I work in ministry, he opened up and said, "I look at my life, and it seems I have it all. I have a good job that brings in good money. I have a beautiful family—a wife and kids. I often find myself, though, looking at all this, wondering, *Why do I feel something is missing? Why do I feel like something feels off?*"

This man felt that he was alone in asking these questions, but I knew he had plenty of company. His confession echoes the desires I hear voiced in my work as a spiritual director and retreat facilitator. I sit with people of all ages who are seeking a relationship with someone in which they understand that they are worthy of love, a relationship that helps them make meaning out of life and that walks with them through their joys and struggles.

These desires are mine too. As a woman, wife, parent, writer, spiritual director, and retreat facilitator, how often I hear myself saying what others say to me! *Something feels missing. I feel empty. I want more, but I am not sure what that means.* My prayer does not always look pretty or sound pretty. I ebb and flow between committed seasons of prayer and seasons where I feel I am barely hanging on in my relationship with God. But this longing we feel—this restlessness that crops up when we know something more is missing—is our hunger for God. Naming these longings and yearnings is a first step we can take in acknowledging that God is already at work within us and in our lives. God is awakening our desire for God.

A Teacher, a Boy, and a Journal

Do you remember when you first felt that missing component in your life?

For me, it came through a jarring conversation with an instructor my junior year of high school. I was raised Catholic. My parents taught me about Jesus and my faith. I went to Catholic school from kindergarten through high school, and the Sisters of St. Joseph taught me about my faith and Jesus. I memorized traditional prayers, checked the length of my skirt so as not to offend Jesus at Mass, and helped crown Mary with flowers. I studied Scripture and knew the basic concepts of the Catholic faith—the Ten Commandments, the Beatitudes, the corporal and spiritual works of mercy.

Then in my junior year of high school came the sacramental prep for my confirmation. Through my parish, I met weekly with a small group of peers and group leaders to discuss our Catholic faith and what it means to be confirmed. In school, the religion class centered on morality. Throughout that year, I attempted to articulate what I believed about my faith and the various teachings of our church.

Yet one day, Ms. Raborn, my religion teacher, looked me square in the eyes and said, "You've missed the boat. You believe whatever your parents believe, and I don't think you can honestly claim any of your beliefs as your own."

This felt like a slap in the face to me—a girl who always tried to look as if she had it together and valued education, critical thinking, and intelligence. I still wince at the memory of it.

Ms. Raborn's challenge, though, served as a wake-up call. She was right: I did not know a darn thing about this faith I proclaimed. More important, I didn't really know God. I knew *about* Jesus and God in the same way people know about me on Facebook, Twitter, or Instagram—knowing a few things about me but not really knowing me. In those places, people know what I let them see and what I have the courage to share. They don't know what makes me tick, who I am, what I long for, what I struggle with, who my friends are, or what God is inviting me to do with my life.

My relationship with God was similar to this. At least from my perspective, we were about as close as distant friends were. I allowed God to see only some aspects of my life, which in reality were the highlights I was most proud of—much like what I choose to post on my social media accounts—such as the times I used my gifts, the moments in my relationships where it was easy to choose love, and the events I felt God would be proud to see. Our relationship seemed to be one where I offered a smattering of thank-yous for the gifts of my life but stayed on the surface otherwise. I acknowledged God as real and as the giver of gifts I had received, but there was not much depth to our interactions, and I did not share myself with God the way I would a close friend.

On the heels of Ms. Raborn's challenge, I was surprised to find that I really did desire a meaningful and vital relationship with God. I wanted to know not just the teachings of my faith but also the Person who was the foundation of that faith. I sensed there was more to this faith than beliefs and teachings—that there was a relationship available to me somehow—and I yearned to experience it.

A month before the senior retreat I described at the beginning of this chapter, I began dating a guy who had begun his own pursuit of faith. As he shared his faith with me, he spoke about knowing God, and it further whet my appetite to start a relationship with God. At Christmas, his gift to me was a journal. In the silence of my room upstairs, I opened the pages of this journal, put pen to paper, and began the journey of exploring the sacred space in me where God resides. Today I can name what I wrote as prayer, but at the time it felt like pouring onto the pages my every thought, question, desire, struggle, and hope.

At the senior retreat the following month, I experienced God in the silence for the first time. But it was coming to God daily in the pages of that journal and my inner, sacred space that I began to know

God. There began a sharing of myself, and the more time I spent in silence, in quiet, in stillness, and in prayer, the more I got to know myself and God. This is how we get to know anyone we consider a friend—by spending time, lots of time, with the other person. Sharing a bit about ourselves with another person helps us understand ourselves better too. At the same time, listening and learning about them deepen our understanding of who they are.

Somehow, in the middle of my sixteen-year-old life that was full of family, friends, school, dating, socializing, applying for colleges, and figuring out how to grow up, God grabbed my heart. It is still mind-boggling to me that it happened, because I didn't set out looking for God or for a relationship with God. In the middle of high school life, my desire for God appeared. But this is how God works. It is God who initiates the relationship and shows up in the middle of ordinary life with all its messiness and beauty, and wakens us up to our desire for God. I didn't even know I was missing a relationship with God until I began building one.

As you read this, you may ask yourself, *Why don't I have a relationship with God?* or *Am I too late?* You may think to yourself, *I've been away for a long time* or *I want to go deeper.* Wherever you are on your faith journey, fear not. Rest assured of this: God desires a true and intimate relationship with you. Pope Francis implores us to understand that God is waiting for us: "When you have the strength to say, 'I want to come home,' you will find the door open. God will come to meet you because he is always waiting for you—God is always waiting for you. God embraces you, kisses you, and celebrates."[2] I invite you now to reflect on your life. Do you notice a sense of restlessness? Do you feel a hunger for something more? Do you desire a relationship with God but don't know where to start? Do you wonder how God can show up in the everyday details of the normal life you live? God

2. Pope Francis, *The Church of Mercy* (Chicago: Loyola Press, 2014), 31.

wants to spend time with us, and we can start sharing that time with God today. Let's turn now to the way that begins.

A Look at Your Life Now

- When do you know something is off in your life? Is it a feeling of unsettledness? anxiety? irritability? restlessness?
- Have you ever had the sense—or do you have the sense now—of God drawing you into relationship or inviting you to deepen your relationship? How did or do you know this?

Assess the areas of your life and your relationships. Does something seem off in any of them? God speaks to us through the restlessness we feel. What might God be saying to you now?

2

Creating Space

The gift of that journal I received at age seventeen first created space for prayer in my life. It was an opening to the dwelling of God within me. Now as an adult, a wife, a mom of three, and a professional, the space I create in my daily life for prayer looks and feels very different from when I was a high school girl writing her thoughts, hopes, and dreams in a hardback, rose-covered journal during stolen moments in her parents' home. Now I seek space within the reality of my life, the busyness of my life, and the fullness of my life and to access that same inner space, God within me. Maybe you can relate.

In my practice of spiritual direction, when I first meet with someone, I ask him or her the following:

> *What is or can be your time of prayer?*
> *Where is or can be your space and place for prayer?*
> *What is or can be your method of prayer?*

Growing in relationship with God means spending time with God. We have to be intentional in making time for what we value most: our family, our friends, and our work. Prayer, too, needs this type of intentionality, and it needs supremacy in our lives. So how do we begin?

Time: Look at your week and your day. When can be your time for prayer? Or when do you find yourself already praying? Are you a morning pray-er? Are you an evening pray-er? Are you a middle-of-the-day pray-er?

Space and Place: Where is your space and place for prayer? Is it inside or outside? Is it in a certain chair in your house? Which room? Is it in your car? Is it in an adoration chapel or church? What things do you want nearby when you pray? For instance, in my space of prayer in my house, I like to have a Bible, a journal, a photo of my kids, and images/items that speak to me about my relationship with God.

Method: What gift of prayer is God giving you at this moment to come to know God? Is it praying with Scripture? Is it music? journaling? the rosary? adoration? Is it simply being quiet and coming to stillness before God? Whatever your method of prayer is at this moment—name it and claim it.

St. Ignatius implores us in his *Spiritual Exercises* to hang on to our space, place, and method of prayer until God exhausts it.[3] All of these will change over time. God will invite us to experience God and get to know God in various places and times and through various avenues. It is to our benefit to listen when the Holy Spirit is inviting us to know God, to notice where the Holy Spirit is inviting us to come to know God, and to recognize through what means we are being invited to get to know God.

Any Time Can Work

First of all, we need to know that we can access God at any time and in any place. We carry a chapel within us—a sacred space—and

---

3. Ignatius of Loyola, *The Spiritual Exercises of St. Ignatius*, trans. Louis J. Puhl (Chicago: Loyola University Press, 1951), 36.

we can call on God at any moment. God is a friend we can talk to throughout the day: as we wake, as we cook, as we eat, as we drive/commute to work, as we play and hang out with our friends. God is available to talk to us as we do laundry, change diapers, run carpool, shuffle kids to activities, oversee homework, and coordinate our families' calendars. *Everything* is holy because our days hold a multitude of ways God can break in and point us back to God as we ponder, pray, and consider.

It's important to remember this because it's easy to be seduced into believing otherwise. For instance, when I look back at the spaces, places, times, and methods of prayer my life has held over time, I see a path speckled with a wide variety of God's gifts. In my late teens and early twenties, I often found myself in front of the Blessed Sacrament in an adoration chapel at a local church in Baton Rouge. I can still close my eyes and hear the quiet, rushing water of the fountains outside that chapel, and I can recall prayer experiences that happened within that chapel as I hungered for respite from the loud experience of communal dorm living.

During those years of prayer, I joined Bible studies and prayer groups offered by Catholic organizations and Campus Crusade for Christ, all of which spoke to my hunger for God and God's invitation to explore faith within a community of people. Both the silence of the adoration chapel and the joyful sharing I experienced among my college peers increased my desire for God and taught me ways to bring more of myself to God and spend more time getting to know Jesus. I experienced huge mountaintop moments of prayer in my late high school and college years, too, as I went on school retreats and participated in a Catholic Leadership Institute, youth conferences, and world youth days.

But as I entered adulthood, the reality of life without the structures of school, clubs, or organizations to help me deepen my faith brought with it a struggle to find a method of prayer that worked for me. I grasped at anything or anyone to show me the way. After a few years of stumbling through life, beating myself up for not being able to make time for adoration, a Bible study, or a prayer group, I realized that my relationship with God did not have to suffer simply because I no longer did these things. Even if my schedule did not align with those activities, I already had everything I needed. Within me, God resides. Within me, God dwells. At any moment and at any time, I can access this interior space.

So that is exactly what I began doing: praying when I could and stopping frequently throughout my day to talk to God and acknowledge God within me. It took some time, but when I let go of the guilt of having to pray a certain way, I realized that I could pray anywhere and at any time. It was freeing to realize that I could grow in my relationship with God in an intimate, personal way without having to show up weekly to a group. Perhaps it will encourage you to hear this as well.

In sharing all this, then, I invite you to stop judging your prayer—to stop beating yourself up about how you are *not* praying and celebrate how you *are*. God is happy to be with you and spend time with you. Yes, there will be invitations to mountaintop experiences of prayer, and there may be time for prayer groups, Bible studies, and retreats at other times. But when the realities of your life do not allow you to participate in those events, you can keep spending time with God. All you have to do is stop and turn your heart and mind to God, talking to God the way you would talk to your closest friend. You have the greatest prayer tool within you—your own sacred space where only you and God reside.

The Space of Thin Places

Let's consider, too, the physical spaces that can help us easily connect to God. William Barry, SJ, in his book *A Friendship Like No Other*, invites us to be aware of our "thin places," those places where we easily find God and can easily name God breaking into our day.[4] I want to offer three ways thin places can show up.

First, there are thin places we may not visit very often but when we do, the felt presence of God is almost overwhelming. Many of mine are places in nature, such as the beach, my grandparents' farm, the North Georgia mountains, and my own garden. These places invite me to understand the vastness and creative power of our Creator. As I stand and soak in the beauty of nature these places offer, I also find that I understand that my mere presence in life is but one piece of God's magnificent, ongoing creative work.

Second, there are basic rhythms and routines that become thin places. For instance, some of my thin places are times I am snuggling with my kids, sipping my morning coffee, sitting down to lunch or a snack with my kids after school to hear about their day, reading to my kids, praying during our nighttime ritual of prayer, and savoring quiet moments with my hubby after the last door of my kids' rooms closes at night. These rhythms of life are spotted with moments that easily allow me to find God. Without realizing it, they have become checkpoints to see how the ones I love are doing. Even more important, they have become "still points" that allow me to savor the gifts in my life and deepen my awareness of God in all things.

Third, certain prayer methods can serve as thin places for us. Prayer methods such as the Examen or Lectio Divina (more to come on these later) can help us silence ourselves and turn to God in prayer. Returning to these prayer methods is like slipping on a worn pair of

---

4. William A. Barry, SJ, *A Friendship Like No Other: Experiencing God's Amazing Embrace* (Chicago: Loyola Press, 2008), 163–76.

favorite jeans. They bring instant comfort and ease, and they often make the return to stillness happen quickly. My mind, body, and heart, without even thinking about it, know that starting one of these prayers readies me to be still and quiet before God and brings me to a deeper place within the reality of my life. Trust me, though—there are certainly days when these methods do not work, because God is inviting me to something else, but these are the go-to methods in my prayer arsenal, and we will learn more about each of them later in this book.

In a way, knowing our thin places sets us up for success in the same way we would start an exercise program, with accountability systems and friends in place, or we would start better eating habits by getting rid of junk food in the pantry and filling the fridge with foods that help us make the right choices. That's what our thin places do. When we know the spaces that help us foster our relationship with God, we are more willing to show up and give prayer our attention.

The Method of Consideration

In addition to knowing our thin places, it is helpful to know some easy methods of prayer. Fr. Joe Tetlow, SJ, suggests that the "prayer of consideration" makes the most sense to those of us who lead busy lives. In this prayer approach, we "raise a mind and heart steeped in concrete circumstances in our life world" to God because, he says, "our minds are filled with perception of friends' needs and children's hopes."[5] Fr. Tetlow suggests that we can pray our days by pausing, acknowledging God within us, and then speaking to God words of thanksgiving or prayers for guidance or help. There are several ways you can use the prayer of consideration throughout your day.

---

5. Joseph A. Tetlow, SJ, *Choosing Christ in the World* (Boston: Institute for Jesuit Sources, 1999), 125.

1. Considering Nature

When I was young, my family went to Philmont Scout Ranch in Cimarron, New Mexico. One of my memories from that trip is my dad wandering off to go stare at the mesa at sunrise and sunset (and probably several other times of day too!). Dad often took a brief moment to stop what he was doing and enjoy the beauty of the mesa.

Taking a "Mesa Moment" is part of my dad's life. I have watched him stop and take in the beauty of his surroundings wherever he is, whether it be in his yard, out his window at work, in my backyard, at the beach, at my grandparents' farm, on a cruise ship, at sunrise, at sunset, or at night. When Dad comes back from his walks or moments of staring, he tends to come back with calmness about him. He also often returns with something new he has gathered—a bird's nest he found on the ground, news of a constellation he saw, a flower that was blooming, or the perfect spot for his grandkids to dig dirt in our backyard. Other times he comes back with a new question to ask or a new insight to share.

I must be honest—there were many days I laughed at Dad for his wandering and staring off into space. However, the older I get, the more I have come to appreciate his Mesa Moments as prayers of consideration. They are prayers in which he considers what God has placed before him and what God is teaching us through what he is noticing. When I follow my dad's example and stop to take a Mesa Moment, I often come back centered and calm too, with a deep appreciation of the beauty and joy God provides.

In our home, I often take these Mesa Moments by noticing what is happening outside my office window, which is in the front of our home. In warmer months, we hang a hummingbird feeder out there, and sometimes I pause while I am writing and notice the birds diving and feeding from it. Sometimes, my children join me in stopping to stare out the window when they get home from school. The tiny creatures fascinate us with their quick speed and lightning-fast wings. They seem in constant motion, flitting from our feeder to the flowers to drink nectar. Often as I watch them, I think about how God created them to be unique creatures with unique gifts. Noticing them, I am reminded of God's creation of me—also unique—and my children and the gifts God gives us, too.

Next time you see something in nature that captivates you, I offer you my dad's example. Stop and take a Mesa Moment, whether it be in your office, on a walk, or in your car. Then consider what God has to teach you then and there.

2. Considering People and Activities

Bill Huebsch writes about the spiritual practice of the "holy pause" in his book *A New Look at Grace*, saying, "This Holy Pause doesn't have to take a lot of time: really two minutes will do it. Pause and ask yourself this question: What has gone on in this time that holds the potential for Mystery?"[6] The Mystery he is referring to is God. Through the holy pause, Huebsch encourages us to stop and consider the common moments in our days, seeking to find God there.

If we practiced the "holy pause" right now, then, what would be revealed about the encounters with God we've had already today? Who have we encountered? What did these encounters teach us about ourselves and about God? What activities have we done today? Where did we feel an increase of faith, hope, and love? What song did we hear that enlivened our soul? Whose words resonated in our core? What book did we read or what show did we watch that spoke to an aspect of our lives? Pausing to consider an ordinary moment is prayer. It is a way of bringing God into daily life.

---

6. Bill Huebsch, *A New Look at Grace: A Spirituality of Wholeness* (New London, Conn.: Twenty-Third Publications, 2003), 22–23.

3. Considering Our Work

Many people spend forty to fifty hours a week at work, and Fr. Tetlow speaks to how the prayer of consideration can be a useful prayer for those in the workforce:

> Those who live busy lives in the marketplace, whose everyday life shifts from merely very full to nearly frantic—they know the value of this prayer. They know that they need time to consider under God's gaze, to ponder and wrangle and exult, to worry with Him and walk with Him.[7]

To practice this, we can ask God for guidance in how we spend the bulk of our week. We can ask God to help us in our interactions with colleagues or with the monotony or the stress within our day. We can seek God's advice and counsel as we make choices and deals and as we evaluate our work ethic. We can thank God for the gift of work and the opportunity to earn money. We can ask God to help us know if we are using our gifts in our job.

In addition, our work, even when not "ministry work," is good and holy work. By way of example, my husband, Chris, is gifted when it comes to math and numbers. Doing math and worrying about the tiniest details of something energizes Chris. He is not called to a professional job in ministry. His skills are best used in a business setting, helping a company reach its goals by paying attention to the small details of numbers and processes. My older brother is a doctor. He knew he wanted to be a doctor since he was in second grade. He is now fully living out his vocation in this work. He is excited and energized and hops out of bed each day, ready to face his work. Both my husband and brother are using the gifts God gave uniquely to them.

---

7. Joseph A. Tetlow, SJ, *Choosing Christ in the World* (Boston: Institute for Jesuit Sources, 1999), 125.

If God picked up the piece of your or my daily work and examined it with us, what would God say? What would we like to cover up and hide? What would we be eager to show God? Asking God these questions can ruffle us a bit sometimes when we get the answers. We may realize we aren't using our gifts or bringing our work to prayer. Maybe we aren't preaching the gospel with our actions at work. Maybe we're not living out a deep dream that God planted within us. As you go about your day at work, pause and turn your heart and mind to God and consider with God what is right in front of you.

4. Considering Our Children

Pondering our children and watching them grow is a common type of prayer for me these days as a mom to three children. My children have much to teach me about God. As I stop to watch them in wonder and as I marvel at who they are in their development and personalities, God often shows me something about myself.

For instance, when my middle daughter, Abby, was a baby, she was a snuggler. I loved this about her! She was totally content being in someone's arms. While she enjoyed playing independently on the ground, sooner or later she would roll, wiggle, or crawl her way right next to me. Once next to me, she would then reach her hands up for me to pick her up, pat her, or hug her. She was not content being too far from us. She wanted to be up in the middle of everything. She wanted to be in one of our laps, being part of what was going on. She wanted eye contact and attention. She desired to be close to me. As her mom, I was happy to oblige her, and I, too, desired this closeness with her.

Pondering this one morning while sitting cross-legged on the floor made me realize that God desires the same thing from me—closeness! God wants to be in a relationship with me. God wants to be close to me. God wants to be invited into the middle of my life, not in a meddling kind of way but in a way that I am inviting God to be part of everything I do. God does not want to miss out on anything, just as Abby does not want to miss out on anything. That is why God is always revealing a part of God to me and always inviting me into a relationship with God. God desires a close relationship with me just as I desire a close relationship with God.

This is how God shows up in our lives and breaks into what feels like a normal day of parenting. Suddenly, *bam!* God has a surprise for me in the middle of sitting on the floor, smelling of spit-up, and counting the minutes until I can get up off the floor and sit in a chair.

With this kind of prayer, stop for a minute and notice your kids. Offer a prayer of thanks to God for their lives and for what God is doing in their lives and within them. What are your kids teaching you about God today?

These are all ways we can pause and bring God into our day, into our routine rhythm of life. Pausing and noticing and considering what God places in front of us brings God to the forefront of our minds and develops within us a heart of gratitude. Like most things in life, the more we practice pausing, noticing, and thanking God for what is in front of us, the easier it will become and the more we will realize how much of our life is already holy.

The Reality of Family Life

Speaking of parenting, I want to pause for a moment and address the parents reading this, especially the moms or other caregivers whose primary role in life right now is tending, nurturing, and raising children. All the time, women ask me, "How do I find time to pray as a mom?"

It is hard to find substantial time to pray when there are little humans that need our constant attention. How can we pray with a babe in our arms or with children bustling around our house? Like all parents, I feel I am constantly evaluating and adjusting my prayer life to fit the new rhythms of our family life. But I've learned a few things along the way.

I try to wake up before my kids do. I sit with a cup of coffee and breathe in the silence and let myself be with God before the rest of the house wakes. Starting my day drinking in God's goodness and presence (along with the beautiful nectar of java!) helps me center my day. It helps me turn my heart and mind to God and start my day with prayer.

Let's be honest, though. There are many days that, despite my best efforts to get up before the kids, they beat me to the punch. My infant daughter wakes earlier than normal and needs to eat. A toddler is frightened by a noise and needs my attention. An older child awakens early for no good reason but is ready to play and begin the day. Or maybe I am just so darn tired that the idea of getting up a few minutes early feels daunting and impossible.

What do I do in these moments?

On many occasions I struggle to know God's invitation for me when I am interrupted by one of my children. I take comfort in the Scripture story of Jesus going off to pray but then, seeing the crowd's needs, taking care of the people. Jesus models for me how to go about my job as a parent, even when it feels hard and as if I'm in the trenches of endless tasks. What I have learned is that Jesus went about his tasks with his Father's help. He carried his cross with God's help. He was deeply established in God, and he turned to God often. He prayed, and then he went about his tasks.

Prayer is vital to building our relationship with God, but there are times when we are simply not capable of giving long periods of prayer to God. I have learned to be okay with this. As one of my former pastors in Baton Rouge would tell me, "Pray as you can, not as you can't!" As parents, we have to pray as we can. We can steal moments of silence for prayer in the early mornings or evenings or during a child's nap or in the middle of our workday or while some of our children are at school. We might find a moment to savor a "holy pause" or a Mesa Moment in nature. We might even find a time in our week to go to daily Mass or to the adoration chapel.

More often than not, though, our best prayer is doing work as parents and turning our hearts and minds to God during our work of the day—as we cook, clean, do laundry, change diapers, potty train, monitor homework time, sit in carpool, shuttle kids to activities, sit on the sidelines at practice or games, and wait for dance lessons to end.

Creating space and time for prayer within family life can be tough. There are five people in my family now, and finding the time, quiet, and space to pray can be very challenging. After years of bumping through my day-to-day life and catching a brief moment of prayer here and there, I finally realized that I needed to let my family—my spouse and the older kids—know what I needed in order to commit to my daily prayer. And what I needed was a few minutes of uninterrupted quiet time.

This felt very awkward for me at first, and at times I felt major guilt about carving out time within my day for prayer. A piece of me felt that I was letting my family down by excusing myself for some time of prayer. When I finally got past the guilt of this and realized that my time with God made me a better wife and mother, it got a heck of a lot easier. It was hard for me, though, to articulate to them what I needed.

To begin with, I have a space for prayer in my house. On most days, I try to do my prayer before everyone is awake or when my older kids are at school and my little one is napping. However, there are days that this beautiful rhythm gets thrown off completely. On those days, with my hubby's help, I let them know I need a few minutes for prayer, and I go sit in my prayer space. And with the noise of the house around me, I pause for a few minutes to be with God. Do I get interrupted? You bet! Is it loud at times? You bet!

While it felt strange for me to do this when everyone was awake, my family, including my kids, honors this space and time for me to be with God. It may not feel like the deepest prayer or my best prayer, but it is prayer, and it serves as a way for me to create space for God within my day and center my life around God. I hope, too, that my kids seeing my husband and me take time to pray will serve as a model for them—that they will come to see this as a normal way of life.

I do want to make one note here, though, about praying within our families. Sometimes when we commit to daily prayer, it ruffles a few feathers. People may not like the changes they see. A dear friend of mine can attest to this. When he made a commitment to his faith and prayer life, his family did not know what to do with him. They saw changes they did not at first understand. They were not on the same faith journey he was. Over time, they understood and respected what he was going through and began their own faith journeys, but the beginning of the process was hard for him.

Sometimes we might find that our families inhibit us in our faith journey instead of support us. We have to make the tough choice of whether to continue on our faith journey when those closest to us are not supportive of it. Maybe they don't understand what's going on. Maybe they don't like the transformation they see. Maybe our desire for a deeper relationship with God makes them uncomfortable because they feel guilty or self-conscious about their own lives and how they are or are not developing faith.

Walking the path of faith, even when the people closest to us do not understand, might be the cost of discipleship. Sometimes the cost is walking a life of faith without the support of our families and loved ones. Over time, though, we hope they will come to see the fruits of our prayer and give us the space we need to continue our faith journey.

The reality is that God wants all of our lives, including our families. We have to ask them for space and a place to pray. This is no different from asking them to help us make time to exercise or pursue a hobby or develop friendships. Our relationship with God needs the support of those around us—our families and other people God puts in our lives to walk with us.

A Look at Your Life Now

- What are some of your "thin spaces"?
- How might you incorporate the prayer of consideration into your daily life?
- What makes, or could make, praying in family life easier? What makes, or could make, praying in family life a challenge?

Try to make a plan for prayer. When could you do it? Where could you do it? And what items or other aids would you want in your prayer space?

3

Beginning of a New Identity

During fall break in my junior year of college, I spent time back home at my parents' house. I remember sitting on my bed and looking up at the walls of my old bedroom. They were adorned with plaques, and my shelves were full of trophies I'd received during my high school years: Religion Award, Leadership Award, PE Award, St. Joseph's Award, Outstanding Graduate. I looked at them with pride, remembering with gratitude those years of high school and the many memories made and friendships formed.

But as I stared at them, I realized that they captured the reality of what once defined me: leadership, academics, faith, running, friendships. It was as if my walls were frozen in time. They still proclaimed the girl I was back then: a girl who was full of energy, who was enthusiastic, who was a leader and a people person, and who made it her relentless pursuit to please others and show that she had it together.

Sitting on my bed that day, I felt as if the awards had not evolved to catch up with the person I was becoming. I sensed that the person I was becoming was defined by something else.

The Consequences of a Faith Life

I want to be real with you. There are consequences to creating space for prayer in your life. If you are looking to keep your life the way it is, then, please, don't pray. If you want to stay the person you currently are, then I suggest not making time for prayer in your daily life. Because here's the reality: If you intentionally show up every day in prayer to be with God, your life is going to change. And guess what else? *You* are going to change!

I am not sharing this to scare you away from prayer but rather to let you know what you can honestly expect if you live a life of prayer. As a spiritual director, I watch this happen again and again. People have the courage to show up and create space in their lives for prayer, and things begin shifting. It can scare the heck out of you as you attempt to make sense of what is going on. But if you are ready for a transformation and ready to live a meaningful life, I invite you to take this leap into deepening your prayer life.

I felt the fruits of my leap into prayer as I looked at my high school trophies that day. I knew they no longer mattered to me as they once had. Even in the infancy of my adult faith, I knew that what defined me was no longer found there. Long before I had the language to name God's love as the catalyst, I knew that I was changing. Things that once mattered and defined who I was were no longer there, or they had changed significantly. I had also, in my early years of college, been exposed to a new world of people who were on fire for their faith. This, alongside my growing prayer life, was shifting what defined me.

Faith That Attracts and Challenges

How did this happen?

Weeks after high school graduation, I attended a Catholic Leadership Institute at Notre Dame University, sponsored by the Diocese of Baton Rouge's Youth Office. For one week, I was surrounded by peers and older adults who were excited about their faith in a way I had never experienced. These people were so full of joy and hope, and they were for real.

I wanted what they had. I wanted their joy, their hope, their confidence, and their authenticity. I could see that their faith was not the kind of inherited faith Ms. Raborn had chastised me for maintaining back in high school. Rather, their faith seemed to be the driving force in their daily lives.

Experiencing people of such faith was like discovering a parallel universe that existed all around me without knowing it was there. I felt both at home and completely lost in this new experience. I sensed an awakening to a new way of being with God, but I also felt clueless about how to proceed. These witnesses of faith modeled a sense of hope and identity that came from somewhere that felt, for me, almost untouchable.

These people were not free of suffering, by any means, but they seemed to live through life's challenges and transitions and joys with a sense of deep hope and the assurance that they would be okay. This seemed to have something to do with their knowing God in a personal way and having a deeper relationship with God than I had yet found.

I was still in the early stages of my journey of faith, but watching this group of people that week, I felt so far away from ever being like them. My faith felt like a new sprout that was not as strong as theirs, and it felt vulnerable and susceptible to being squashed by anything that tested it.

Have you ever felt like that? Like your faith was tiny compared to the magnitude of another person's faith? This experience happened to me as a college student, but a person can experience this same kind of attraction and longing for "something more" at any time and stage of life. Men and women of all ages walk into my office for the first time to meet with me for spiritual direction and name their desire to go deeper without knowing where to start. Often, the catalyst for their coming to meet with me is a life event or the example of a person they've encountered.

Summer of 1998

My newfound faith was invigorated during my time at Catholic Leadership Institute. Shortly after I returned home, though, my world changed drastically. Within a few weeks I was grappling with the loss of one of my dear friend's sisters, who died in a skydiving accident. That same month, we learned that a high school friend had an inoperable brain tumor. As my freshman year in college began, I also told the guy I was dating good-bye as he left for college in another state and I entered the world of dorm life. These events opened me to a world of loss, doubt, suffering, hurt, change, and questions. At the same time, I was attempting to nurture along a relationship with God that had been nudged forward by the witness of the people I met at Catholic Leadership Institute.

I was finding that all that used to define me no longer worked. I was not the articulate, put-together girl who had all the answers. I could no longer define myself by the things I used to be and do in high school. Dorm living left me with little time to myself, and I was thrown into a new world of exploration and discovery and freedom. I did not even feel right claiming to be Catholic because everything I once believed didn't make sense anymore. I felt a deep disconnect was growing between what I knew about God and what it meant to know God.

I can't say that I would choose to relive that season of spiritual growth; it rocked me to my core. It's likely that you, too, have experienced at least one moment like this, in which everything that once defined you no longer existed. I wish I could say that time in college was the only time it happened to me, but even in the most recent

decade of my life, I can name multiple moments that created a similar dynamic—a change in the roles I played or in the relationships
I held, or a complete upheaval of my physical location that left me
whirling, wondering who I was and what I could hold on to. These
changes have become easier to manage over the years as my identity
has become more attuned to the woman I am before God rather than
circumstances or relationships.

Fortunately, though, this journey of faith is never a journey of isolation. At the same time my world was falling apart and I was losing
a sense of who I was, people showed up who pointed the way to base
my identity on simply being a woman of God. It was with their help,
witness, and encouragement that I began rebuilding my life on this
foundation.

A Cuban Nun

One day at Mass at the Christ the King parish on my college campus,
I heard an announcement for a "busy-person's retreat." I thought,
Hmm . . . well, I am a busy person. (Or at least I thought I was at the
time, balancing school, part-time work, dating, and a social life—oh,
if I could talk to that version of myself now to tell her what busyness
really is!)

I signed up, having no idea what I was getting myself into. Then I
received an e-mail telling me I would be assigned a spiritual director.
At the time, I had no idea what a spiritual director was. What would
I talk to her about? How was this going to work?

Enter Sr. Ily, a beautiful Sister of St. Joseph who had a Cuban
accent and a warm, loving heart. She and I met on the opening day of
the busy-person's retreat, and she explained to me the process. Each
day, I would spend an hour in prayer, and then she and I would meet
for one hour each day as well, to discuss what had happened during

my prayer. I remember flipping out, asking her, "What do I do in my prayer time?"

She suggested I try praying with Scripture. Even as I type this, I feel as if I want to let loose a drum roll or blast some horns to announce the major gift this became for me. Sr. Ily taught me how to pray with Scripture through this busy-person's retreat.

Keep in mind that I went to Catholic schools for years K–12. I had heard a ton of Scripture. Even one of the religion courses I took in high school was a year spent on Scripture. In those thirteen years, though, no one had ever taught me how to *pray with Scripture*.

Sr. Ily walked me through how to do this—and I will walk you through how to do this, as well, in chapter 5—and then she assigned me Psalm 139 to use in my prayer.

When I read the words of Psalm 139, they pierced right through me:

> O LORD, you have searched me and known me.
> You know when I sit down and when I rise up;
> you discern my thoughts from far away.
> You search out my path and my lying down,
> and are acquainted with all my ways.
>
> Even before a word is on my tongue,
> O LORD, you know it completely.
> You hem me in, behind and before,
> and lay your hand upon me.
> Such knowledge is too wonderful for me;
> it is so high that I cannot attain it.
>
> Where can I go from your spirit?
> Or where can I flee from your presence?
> If I ascend to heaven, you are there;
> if I make my bed in Sheol, you are there.
> If I take the wings of the morning

and settle at the farthest limits of the sea,
even there your hand shall lead me,
and your right hand shall hold me fast.

If I say, "Surely the darkness shall cover me,
and the light around me become night,"
even the darkness is not dark to you;
the night is as bright as the day,
for darkness is as light to you.

For it was you who formed my inward parts;
you knit me together in my mother's womb.
I praise you, for I am fearfully and wonderfully made.
Wonderful are your works;
that I know very well.
My frame was not hidden from you,
when I was being made in secret,
intricately woven in the depths of the earth.
Your eyes beheld my unformed substance.
In your book were written
all the days that were formed for me,
when none of them as yet existed.
How weighty to me are your thoughts, O God!
How vast is the sum of them!
I try to count them—they are more than the sand;
I come to the end—I am still with you.

O that you would kill the wicked, O God,
and that the bloodthirsty would depart from me—
those who speak of you maliciously,
and lift themselves up against you for evil!

Do I not hate those who hate you, O Lord?
And do I not loathe those who rise up against you?
I hate them with perfect hatred;
I count them my enemies.

Search me, O God, and know my heart;
test me and know my thoughts.
See if there is any wicked way in me,
and lead me in the way everlasting. (Ps. 139)

Who was this God—one who knows me and understands me, from whose presence I cannot hide or flee, who formed my inmost being? How was it that an entity like this exists—and why did I not know this about God until now?

I immediately knew I wanted to be in a relationship with someone from whom I could not hide and who loved me despite any and all my flaws. This lit a fire inside me—similar to the fire that ignited when Ms. Raborn told me I had missed the boat in defending my faith. Praying with Scripture like this opened a whole new world for me. I not only wanted to know the God who knew me like this but also wanted to grow in my relationship with God on a daily basis.

The busy-person's retreat came to an end, and I continued to pray with Scripture. This became my method of prayer. My place of prayer was my room in the sorority house—but I fumbled my way through finding a time and space that worked with my calendar and provided me the quiet I yearned for while living with a roommate's bed five feet from my own. At times, I would pray while my roommate was gone or was sleeping. Other times, I would take my journal, Bible, and pen to another location, such as an adoration chapel or church. My hunger for this quiet, contemplative prayer with Scripture continued to grow. I began to embrace my inner chapel more and more. As I did this, my relationship with God and my understanding of what it means to be a woman of God continued to grow.

What Defines You?

How simple it would be to boil ourselves down to our roles, our accomplishments, and our relationships! Right now I could sum up my main roles as wife, mother, spiritual director, writer, and retreat facilitator. I might go on to add my role in my extended family or the fact that I am a huge LSU fan or that I am from South Louisiana. All these pieces of my life are important to me. What list would describe you?

What would hang on your walls and adorn your bookshelves, defining who you are or showing a stranger a glimpse of what you are about, if you had such a wall of accomplishments? Would people see pieces of your job? your career? your possessions? your successes? your roles as parent, daughter/son, grandchild, aunt/uncle, cousin, friend? Would your walls boast about your children and their accomplishments, as my fridge does, with its display of colorful art projects and treasures made by my kids? Might there be a memory of an important event or a voice from your past that had an impact on you? What about the hidden pieces of your life—the ones you may not hang on your wall but are part of your life's story too, the quiet, life-defining moments that change you for the good or bad? If you, too, were to sit back and look at the evidence of your life collected on your wall, what might you find there that's defining who you are?

I notice in others and in myself the search for something constant and consistent. We are looking for someone or something to assure us of our worth and value. At times, we look to our jobs or our salaries to affirm us. Other times, we feel secure because of what we've accomplished or the affirmations we've received from others. Maybe we define ourselves by where we live and what we own. I have watched myself and others place our entire sense of our worthiness in our families or our children; we feel a sense of value and security as we survey the stable environment we've created for our families.

What happens, though, when one of these things changes or when the very thing that defined us no longer exists? Maybe we lose our job, or a relationship ends or changes. Maybe our family environment goes from calm to churning. Maybe we lose a loved one or experience loss of health. Maybe we experience something that hurts or wounds us. Maybe we relocate physically and everyone we once knew is now miles away. How, then, do we define ourselves? Where do we find solid footing?

If the essence of who we are is tied to what we do, what we own, what we have accomplished, or who we are in relationship with, we are in for a world of sadness and disappointment. If there is one thing I've learned in the past two decades of life, it is that change and transition are ongoing but that God, no matter our circumstances, remains constant.

Receiving a New Identity

Several months after the busy-person's retreat and the beginning of my new practice of praying with Scripture, I found myself sitting on my bed in my parents' home, staring at that wall of trophies and awards. Life had thrown some unexpected things my way since I'd won them, and my worldview and sense of self were changing. I saw that clinging to those tangible signs of my old identity was costing me. It was costing me my voice, my gifts, and my very self. I was restless, unfulfilled in my search to please and satisfy all those around me.

My former English teacher, Ms. Simmons, had posted on her board all year, "You cannot please all the world and one's Father." I realized that I could not please God and the entire world at the same time. It costs all of us, actually, when we tie our identity into being defined by someone or something else.

And so I stood and took down every one of those trophies and awards and plaques. I boxed them up, sealed the lid, and put them on a shelf in my closet. I was not—and still am not—ashamed of the awards by any means, but I felt they could no longer hang on the wall,

tempting me to hold tightly to what they represented instead of clinging to God.

My dad, to this day, asks me about that day I cleared the wall of my
old room. As a parent now, I cannot imagine what it would be like to
watch this happen with one of my own children. What I tell him, I
can also tell you: This was a mile marker for me, a huge step toward
coming to know my authentic self—the woman I am in God.

First Principle and Foundation

In chapter 5, I will share with you in detail the method of praying
with Scripture that Sr. Ily taught me and how you can use it in your
daily life. For now, I want to focus on a key piece of learning that
I began to understand around that same time and that I find useful
today when walking with others in spiritual direction as they commit
to creating space for prayer. It is captured in a meditation St. Ignatius
put at the beginning of his *Spiritual Exercises*, called the First Principle
and Foundation. It reads:

> The goal of our life is to live with God forever.
> God, who loves us, gave us life.
> Our own response of love allows God's life
>   to flow into us without limit.
>
> God who loves us creates us and wants to
>   share life with us forever.
> Our love response takes shape in our praise and
>   honor and service of the God of our life.
>
> All the things in this world are also created
>   because of God's love
> And they become a context of gifts,
>   presented to us so that we can know God more easily
> and make a return of love more readily.

As a result, we show reverence for all these gifts of creation
and collaborate with God in using them
    so that by being good stewards
We develop as loving persons in our care of God's world
    and its development.
But if we abuse any of these gifts of creation or,
    on the contrary, take them
As the center of our lives,
    we break our relationship with God
And hinder our growth as loving persons.

In everyday life, then, we must hold ourselves in balance
before all of these created gifts insofar as we have a choice
and are not bound by some responsibility.
We should not fix our desires on health or sickness,
wealth or poverty, success or failure, a long life or short one.
For everything has the potential of calling forth in us
a more loving response to our life forever with God.
Our only desire and our one choice should be this:
I want and I choose what better
leads to the deepening of God's life in me.[8]

St. Ignatius teaches us through this First Principle and Foundation that there are many gifts in our world: relationships, jobs, income, families, and more. But when we let any of these gifts become the center of life, we displace God. From experience, I can tell you that when God is knocked out of the center, we feel restless, unsettled, and empty—basically the opposite of what most of us seek, which we might name as peace, fulfillment, or meaning.

Through the First Principle and Foundation, Ignatius invites us to live in a stance of *detachment*. What in the world does he mean by

---

8. David L. Fleming, SJ, *Draw Me into Your Friendship: The Spiritual Exercises*
(St. Louis, Mo.: Institute of Jesuit Sources, 1996), 27.

that word? In my mind, I boil it down to this: God wants to be the center of our lives. It is in God and God alone that we find our worth and value. At the same time, God gives us gifts. As humans, we have a tendency to center ourselves on these gifts. St. Ignatius teaches us to be detached from the gifts God gives us—not to put our stock or our value in the gifts but in the giver of the gifts. All of the gifts God gives us—our work, our family, our friends, the place we live—have the potential to help us grow deeper in our relationship with God, but we must hold them in balance, with our life centered on God. In this way, we are "detached" from the gifts because we are mindful of what they truly are: gifts from God, given to us to grow deeper in God and for us to help others grow deeper in God.

This movement toward detachment is what I felt as I looked at those trophies and awards on my old bedroom wall. God was slowly dethroning those gifts from the center of my life and placing God's self in the center instead. I was learning to seek my worth in God rather than in awards, leadership positions, or accomplishments—and God used not only the events of my life but also my prayer to help this shift occur.

Knotted Beauty

That season of life taught me that prayer happens within the reality of life, not apart from it. One is not separate from the other. This is why Ignatian spirituality was and is so fitting to me; it seeks to find God in *all things*, not just in church. Faith is not a separate category of our lives; rather, it is woven into the fabric of our very being. Life and prayer have an impact on one another. That's the knotted beauty of the summer of 1998 and my college years. Life and faith were happening at the same time—one growing on the other, one using the other to wrap and strengthen and propel its growth, life and faith working simultaneously to help me turn toward God as the center and source of my life.

My guess is that God is doing the same for you. Using your life and your desire to move God to the center of your life, God is making *every part* of your life holy. This is why creating space for prayer is a risk worth taking: it creates space for you to know the person God sees: a beautiful man or woman loved by God.

It helps, though, to develop eyes to notice and see God at work. That is what we will turn our attention to learning next.

A Look at Your Life Now

- What would hang on your wall right now that defines you? Are any of these roles and relationships changing? If all these went away, what would define you then?

- As you look at your life, are any of the gifts of your life at the center, rather than the Giver of the gifts?

- Who are people in your life whose lived example of faith attracts you to the faith? What is attractive about their example?

1. Read the First Principle and Foundation on page 35.

2. Write down the word or phrase that captures your attention.

3. Reflect on what you feel God is saying to you in this/ through this.

4. Name some of your gifts you might be invited to detach from at this time.

4

Living Awake

I am from Baton Rouge, Louisiana, and lived there when Hurricane Katrina hit. My husband and I were okay, and our home was okay. We did not deal with the direct impact of rising water, the flood, or the loss of our home. However, very close family members and friends in New Orleans and Baton Rouge were affected dramatically, and the intensity of watching them hurt so much was gut-wrenching. In an instant, their lives were forever changed.

The utter chaos that surrounded Baton Rouge and nearby New Orleans left me confused and angry. All the hurt, pain, and loss brought me to a place where I questioned God and felt extremely helpless. In addition, I was working in the Christian Formation Office at the Diocese of Baton Rouge, and I witnessed people lining up all day outside Catholic Charities. People came into our hallway asking for help to find their families, recover their possessions, or get back on their feet. We did all we could. Nothing we did seemed adequate, though. Often all we could do was point people to the services across the parking lot, where people armed with tools, knowledge, and resources that we didn't have could offer them more help than we could.

But everyone in South Louisiana did all they could to help. We opened our homes to strangers. We sat with family and friends and sometimes strangers and let them talk and cry. We helped family and friends move and unpack their belongings. We sat in silence with people as they grieved the loss of entire lives: home, city, possessions, work, friends, church, school. People lost all that was familiar to them.

I felt that I was being swallowed up by all the suffering around me. Everywhere I looked, there was sadness and despair. Everywhere I looked, I saw the lasting impact of a natural disaster. I did not understand how it happened. I did not understand why God would let this happen. To be honest, I still do not know the answer. People were turning to me as a person in ministry, asking me to answer the very questions I was asking myself. *How did God let this happen? Where was God in all this?*

It was this life experience and these questions of faith that I brought with me eight months later to the Cenacle Retreat House nestled on the shores of Lake Pontchartrain in New Orleans for my annual silent retreat. Driving to the retreat house from Baton Rouge, I could still see signs of Katrina's long-lasting damage. Blue tarps on roofs spotted the horizon. Uprooted trees and belongings littered front lawns, moldy and ruined, haphazardly piled together in someone's effort to clean up.

I entered the retreat house's property and felt the same calming presence I normally felt when I entered this sacred space, but it was impossible not to think of what I had just seen on my drive. So before checking in, I parked my car and walked across the huge front lawn and out the gate that separates the retreat house from Lake Pontchartrain's levee.

I climbed to the top of the levee, and what I saw took my breath away. It was a beautiful April day with a blue sky and very little wind. The lake stood before me, calm and still. The irony of the moment hit me hard. Here I was, breathing in the beauty of the moment, overlooking a calm, still lake that months before was raging against the very levee I stood upon, the waves crashing against it and filling the canals to the point of bursting, causing a flood unlike anything New Orleans had ever seen.

Standing in that silent moment, I felt my sadness, grief, anger, and questions rise up. *How did this happen, God? How does healing happen? Where are you? What am I called to do?* I stood there several minutes, noticing the beauty of the day but also unable to ignore the raging storm of questions, anger, and helplessness.

Then, with a tired but hopeful heart, I walked back down the levee, across the huge lawn, and through the doors of the retreat house to begin my forty-eight hours of silence.

✝

Fr. Matt Linn, SJ, directed our retreat that weekend. Fifty women gathered inside the retreat house—fifty women from Southern Louisiana who had just lived through Hurricane Katrina. I cannot imagine the responsibility Fr. Matt must have felt, knowing his call to minister to us that weekend. As it was, it quickly became clear that the group would have a hard time respecting the silence. We needed to talk. I will never know if Fr. Matt intended to teach us what he did that weekend or if he just saw our need for it, but Saturday afternoon he gave a talk on the Examen—a type of prayer that helps us notice God's presence in the events of our days—and then invited us to pray the Examen and share our responses.

What happened was a moment of naming the ways God was present and had been present in the middle of Hurricane Katrina. People voiced their pain and struggles. Many there had lost everything. Some had been in New Orleans during Katrina. All of us had felt its impact in some way.

The release I felt that afternoon is hard for me to capture with words. It was through praying the Examen that I could name for the first time God at work despite the suffering I saw on a daily basis. I was able to name God at work in the way people stepped up to help others. People welcomed family and friends into their homes to live. People welcomed strangers into their homes to stay. People gave money and time and goods and whatever they could. Eight months later, people still were giving. Church parishes adopted other churches and welcomed parishioners so they could find people they knew. Schools opened their doors to students from New Orleans. Some schools even allowed high schools from New Orleans to have complete run of their campuses at night so the displaced students could experience some sense of normalcy.

On that retreat, I also named God in the courageous efforts of people such as my sister-in-law, a nurse who stayed behind and weathered the storm in a hospital in New Orleans, taking care of eleven ICU patients. She was the hardest for me to watch in the months after Katrina. I have never felt so helpless as I did when I sat with her, listening to her stories of that time in the hospital. I wanted to take away her pain and her experience of the storm. I could not believe God would allow someone to hurt as deeply as she did. To this day, I cannot answer why God let it happen to anyone. All I know is that it did happen and that the long-lasting effects of Hurricane Katrina are still there, both in the region itself and in the lives of people who live there.

That day I first prayed the Examen, I found God bringing to mind, through the example of my sister-in-law, the way God uses people to do God's work on this planet. Her witness reminded me of this prayer attributed to St. Teresa of Avila:

> Christ has no body now but yours,
> No hands, no feet on earth but yours,
> Yours are the eyes with which he looks

Compassion on this world,
Yours are the feet with which he walks to do good,
Yours are the hands, with which he blesses all the world.
Yours are the hands, yours are the feet,
Yours are the eyes, you are his body.

Being able to name God at work in the middle of this awful disaster brought freedom. It brought hope to see God working through others, comforting each person as he or she cried out to God for help. It brought me peace to see God grieving for the pain and heartache as much as I did.

At the same time, praying the Examen that day helped me bring before God all the places I struggled to see God at work. I brought before God my question of why Katrina happened in the first place. My heart poured out questions such as, *Why did you seem to abandon some and save others? Why did you let this happen?* It was freeing to bring such raw, honest prayer to God. I felt heard, the way Jesus must have felt in the Garden of Gethsemane when he begged God to the point of sweat coming out like blood, "Remove this cup from me" (Luke 22:42).

At the end of the silent retreat, Fr. Matt asked us to write down something we learned on retreat that we wanted to bring back into our normal lives. I wrote that I wanted to begin praying the Examen. Starting the Monday I returned home, then, I began praying it daily.

My prayer felt clunky at first, as though I were learning to ride a bike for the first time. Even with the steps written out in front of me (which I will share on pages 45–47), it felt strange to bring all of my life before God. I struggled to believe that God cared about all the tiny details of my life. But what I discovered was that all the tiny details of my life *do* matter to God. More important, all those tiny details refined my skill of noticing all the ways God shows up in my days. It developed my understanding that God truly can be found in all things.

I cannot imagine where I would be today without the Examen. Using this prayer method for the past ten years, I can say that this little prayer has brought much fruit to my life. I understand why St. Ignatius told his brother Jesuits, *If you pray any prayer at all this day, pray the Examen.*

Finding God in the Past Twenty-Four Hours

So, what is the Examen? In a nutshell, it is a method of prayer that you normally complete at the end of your day—it takes about ten to fifteen minutes—that involves praying about the past twenty-four hours of your life. You look with God at the pieces of your life, one by one, as though you were examining the pieces of a puzzle.

To share with you more of what this means, I'll give you an example from my home. My kids and I like to do puzzles. Many days, after completing one puzzle, we bring another one out. On one such day, we had multiple puzzles out, and we decided it was time to clean up. So we did, carefully placing each puzzle back in its appropriate box. But as my daughter grabbed the boxes to bring them upstairs, the boxes slipped out of her hands, dumping the puzzles into a heap, the different puzzles mixing together. So Abby and I sat down and began examining the pieces together, hoping to get them sorted into their right boxes.

One by one, we would look at a puzzle piece and examine its color, shape, and size. We would ask, "Where does this belong?" It was easy to determine where some pieces belonged, but others were more difficult to figure out. We had to sit with those a bit longer and examine them more closely. Eventually, we finished the job.

This is often how I picture praying the Examen. Jesus is sitting down next to me, and together we are picking up the pieces of the

past twenty-four hours of my life and examining them. We are looking at everything that occurred in those twenty-four hours. With the
Holy Spirit's help, I can review those hours and see where I can give
thanks and name God's presence. At the same time, with the Holy
Spirit's help, I can see where I struggled to name God or did not act
as I wanted. Together, Jesus and I are asking, "Does this belong? Does
this help me grow closer in my relationship with God?" Then, after
we look at the pieces of my day, I look to my next twenty-four hours
and ask for God's help with it.

Typically, there are five steps to the Examen. The organized plan-
ner that I am really likes that there are five steps—that when I complete one, I can move on to the next, and then the next, and then the
next until my prayer is complete. And while there are five simple steps
to the Examen, what occurs in this small prayer is quite powerful. It is
not simply a process of running through a memorized prayer, spout-
ing off words without much thought or purpose. Rather, it is a prayer
of intentional reflection on your day that literally involves bringing
your entire life before God and praying about it.

So, what are the steps?

The Five Steps of the Examen

The Examen's five simple steps are as follows:

1. Ask for the Holy Spirit's help.

In this step, you place yourself in the presence of God and ask the
Holy Spirit to help you see your day as God sees it. Often my step
one sounds something like this: "Holy Spirit, give me your eyes to see
my day, your ears to understand my day, your heart to view my day."

2. Be thankful.

Look back over your past twenty-four hours, and name all that you
are thankful for: the people you encountered within the past day,

something inspiring or encouraging that you witnessed, a pleasure you enjoyed such as a good meal, the people who love you, such as family and friends. With Jesus' help, name all the gifts and thank God for them.

3. Notice God's presence.

Look backward over your day, hour by hour, and name where you felt an increase of faith or hope or love. Be specific about what you were doing and whom you were with when this happened. Notice what was happening within you as you recall each moment of your day. Here are some examples:

- a meaningful conversation with someone
- a moment at work when you really enjoyed what you were doing
- a song you heard or book you read or TV show you saw
- something you saw in nature
- a line of Scripture or a prayer

Look over your day and identify when you felt the fruit of the Spirit. Try to be mindful of what you were doing when you felt the fruit of love, joy, peace, patience, kindness, generosity, faithfulness, gentleness, or self-control. What is God saying to you in these moments?

4. Notice the lack of God's presence.

Look backward again over your day, hour by hour, and identify where you felt a decrease in faith, hope, or love. Be specific about what you were doing when you noticed this decrease. Ask, Why did I experience a decrease in faith, hope, or love at that moment? You can follow up with the following questions:

- Did I not choose love?
- Did I not act the way I wanted?

- Did God seem absent or hidden in these moments? Why? Was it because of my choice or action? Another person's choice or action?
- Why am I struggling to name God in these moments?
- What is God saying to me about them?

In this step, ask God's forgiveness for the places where you chose not to love or act the way you wanted.

5. Look to the future.

Turning to your next twenty-four hours, ask God to give you what you need for your tasks and responsibilities in those hours. Resolve that, with God's grace, you will do better tomorrow in certain areas than you did today. Then close your prayer with an Our Father.

The Graces of the Examen

The Examen is a prayer often credited to St. Ignatius but was possibly around before his time. Ignatius was adamant that his brother Jesuits do this prayer every day. I understand why he would put such value on it. It has helped me remain a woman of prayer over the past ten years, and it continues to be one of my go-to prayer methods through which I can easily and readily meet God. It has brought many gifts into my life.

For one thing, I never run out of anything to speak to God about when it comes to this prayer. I always have the day to review with God. All my relationships are brought before God, as are all my jobs and roles and responsibilities. Like the prayer of consideration, the Examen is a prayer of simply placing yourself before God, turning your mind and heart to God, and reviewing your day with the Spirit's help.

Praying the Examen also develops the grace of awareness. Through this prayer, we discover that God can be found in all things and all moments—even moments such as Hurricane Katrina that seem to be suffused with suffering. The Examen helps us wake up to see God at work through other people, through events, work, gifts and talents, music, books, nature, and our church communities.

The world seems alive and vibrant to me after years of praying the Examen. Often I look out my window and can sense immediately that everything is holy. I am aware of God working in my life. The Examen fosters my ability to notice God in all things.

How, then, do we go about developing the ability to notice God active, involved, and present in our lives? I suggest we start by praying the Examen! Find a ten-minute time slot in your day; maybe it's morning or evening. Or maybe it's somewhere in the middle of your day. One woman, a mother of six whom I met for spiritual direction, found time to pray the Examen in her driveway after dropping two of her high school children at their sports practice. Before the garage doors would roll up, signaling to the rest of the family that she was home, she would put her car in park and sit for ten minutes in silence and pray the Examen. She saw the fruit of this prayer quickly; it helped her notice God at work, helped her foster a spirit of gratitude for the gifts of her life, and helped her honestly bring before God the entirety of her daily experience. That's what the Examen does: It helps us refine the art of noticing God at work in ordinary life, today. What about you? Where might you find a time and a place to pray the Examen each day?

The amazing thing is, as we come to see, through the Examen, the concrete ways God is intimately involved in our lives, we begin to awaken to the depths to which God loves us. Let's turn now to explore those depths.

A Look at Your Life Now

- Is there a "storm" in your history or that you are going through now that makes it hard to notice God at work? Describe that storm in words or in a drawing so that you can look at it.

- What or who makes it easy to notice God's presence? What or who makes it difficult to notice God in everyday life?

Find ten minutes in your day and commit to praying the Examen every day for a week.

5

Awakening to God's Love

When Chris and I first started dating, we were juniors in college. We had known each other since high school, and we were friends all through high school and college. It's funny, when I look back, I realize that Chris was always around, much as God is, but it wasn't until junior year of college that we began to see each other as more than friends. Just as we one day wake up and recognize God in our lives and our hunger for a relationship with God, the same happened for me with Chris. One day I realized that I had an interest in him beyond that of a friend.

Our first date was a few months after the busy person's retreat I spoke about in chapter 3. Our date consisted of dinner and a movie, and after the movie ended, we talked into the wee hours of the night. As he walked me to my door, I knew there was something different about that night—something I had not felt before.

The next day, I was heading out of town for a spring-break trip to Chicago. As I thought about the previous night's date, I found myself wanting to see Chris again before being gone a week. I chuckle at this now, but I actually called him and asked to borrow a book sack for my trip (because clearly I did not have one of my own, even though I used one every day for class—ha!). He, too, said he "needed" to borrow a DVD from me. We met briefly Friday afternoon and traded our borrowed items. After this second encounter in his presence, I knew something was different from how things used to be.

I went away for a week, and I found myself thinking about Chris quite often. I was eager to return home and spend time with him again. When I returned, we fell quickly into a dating relationship, and we spent a ton of time together. Everything was so new and exciting. There were so many things to learn about each other. We took every opportunity we could to be together. Over time, we began to realize the love we had for each other.

How did Chris and I get to know each other and come to understand our love for each other? Simple: by spending time together. The more time we spent together, the more I found myself willing to open up to him, talk to him, and share another piece of my life's story with him. He, too, opened up to me.

Chris loved all of me, including my gifts, my strengths, and my weaknesses. He accepted all my unique qualities. He accepted all of me. I did not show him everything at first, but over time, as we got to know each other more, I let myself become more vulnerable with him. With every risk I took, he met that opening with arms of love. These interactions, which numbered into the hundreds over the year and a half we dated, increased our understanding of each other and our love for each other. Over time, we learned that we loved each other for who we were and not for who we were not.

Awakening to God's love for us and our love for God unfolds much as a human romance and other meaningful relationships: slowly and over time. When we start out in our relationship with God, it may feel new, different, and exciting. And as we continue to show up and make space for God, we become more comfortable with God, and we get to know God better. We also allow God to know more of us (even though God already sees all of us!). Over time, the relationship grows, just as any friendship or significant relationship does. It goes through bumps and bruises, highs and lows, joys and pains, dry periods and periods of immense growth. Eventually, we learn to trust God enough that we can bring our true selves—the people we are, not the people we are not—to God. As Fr. Tetlow reminds us in his book *Making Choices in Christ*:

> You are who God wants you to be. God loves you as you are—not as you might be or could be. God loves you because you are who you are, for God is making you who you are. When you know this, you have accepted the most intimate relationship with God that a busy life allows, a relationship that fills all things.[9]

It wasn't easy to let God love me as I was. And from years spent listening to other people talk about their experiences in their relationships with God, I can tell you this is one of the most difficult parts of our faith journey: understanding the depths to which we are loved by God.

I wish there were an easy answer or solution to give you so that you could grasp this concept deep in your bones right now. However, the only honest suggestion I can give you is this: show up and spend time with God. That is the basis of this entire book, really—encouraging you to make time for God on a daily basis. Why do I want to tell you to do this and offer helpful ways for you to cultivate space for God? Because hanging out with God in prayer on a regular basis transformed my life, and I have seen it transform the lives of so many others too.

Nothing is more important or foundational than our understanding of God's love for us. It's the premise and the foundation on which the rest of our understanding of God is based. There is a reason St. Ignatius called the first meditation in the *Spiritual Exercises* the First

---

9. Joseph A. Tetlow, SJ, *Making Choices in Christ: The Foundations of Ignatian Spirituality* (Chicago: Loyola Press, 2008), 15.

Principle and Foundation—because understanding God's love for us is foundational to our faith. If we do not understand God's love for us, then we find it hard to trust, to believe in God's mercy. It's hard to accept God's forgiveness; it's hard to follow Jesus; it's hard to believe we are uniquely called to be part of God's mission; it's hard to have hope and joy. God's love is foundational.

Let's turn now to a prayer tool that can help us awaken to God's love for us.

Lectio Divina

Lectio Divina is a method of praying the Scriptures. What better way to get to know God than by spending time with God's spoken word?

The practice of Lectio Divina traces its roots back to the early centuries in the Church. By the sixth century, St. Benedict had made it a regular practice in most monasteries. And while in its beginnings this prayer method was set aside for monks and religious, today Lectio Divina is a widely held practice by many laymen and laywomen. I teach this method of prayer to people on retreats and in my ministry of spiritual direction.

Lectio Divina is a slow, rhythmic reading and praying of a Scripture passage. You pick a passage and read it. Notice what arises within you as you read it. Then you read it again, and then again, noticing what words and phrases grab your heart and noticing the feelings that arise. You respond to God about whatever is stirring within as you read and pray with the passage. Finally, you rest and let God respond and speak to you.

Let's consider the formal steps. To begin, you might open with a short prayer, asking God to guide your prayer time. Then do the following:

Read.

Slowly and thoughtfully, read the Scripture passage the first time. What word or phrase captures your attention and grabs your heart? Linger with it whenever this happens.

Reflect.

Slowly and prayerfully, read the passage again. What is God saying to you in this passage? offering you? asking you? What feelings are arising within you?

Respond.

Slowly and prayerfully, read the passage again. Respond to God from your heart. Speak to God of your feelings and insights. Offer these to God.

Rest.

Possibly read the passage another time. Sit quietly in God's presence, asking, "What are you saying to me?" Rest in God's love, and listen.

As you end your prayer period, you might close with an Our Father or another short prayer. It might be helpful to jot down in a journal what arose during this time. What did you speak to God, and what did God offer you?

How do you know what Scripture passages to use? One way is to literally flip through the Bible until you find something that catches your attention. (I call this the Russian-roulette method.) Another way is to find a Scripture passage that you already know and like. For instance, I frequently use Philippians 4:4–9; Psalm 1; and Psalm 139. There's also a multitude of Scripture resources that offer the daily readings. The United States Conference of Catholic Bishops' website (www.usccb.org), for instance, lists the daily Scriptures online. Other resources, such as Give Us This Day or the Magnificat, offer a monthly book in the mail with the daily Mass readings, a reflection, and a word of wisdom from a saint or about a saint. Devotionals of all kinds offer an intentional way of praying with Scripture, sometimes by season (such as Advent or Lent) or specifically for women or men or mothers or fathers. By doing a little research online or stopping at a local bookstore, you can find a resource to support this practice of praying with Scripture in this way. This may be a prayer tool you use occasionally at the beginning or it may become part of your daily prayer.

Lectio Divina offers a particular way of growing in awareness of God through God's living word. Scripture captures our salvation history, from Adam and Eve to Jesus to the disciples to us. It shows us the work of God throughout history, and the words of God for others in history still have meaning for us today.

Eventually, after praying with Scripture enough and encountering through Scripture the truths that we are created in God's image and likeness and that, because God created us, we are innately good, we begin to believe these truths. They begin to sink in and take permanent root in our thinking. It is the deepening of our understanding of God's love for us that ultimately transforms us. Like any relationship, it takes hearing it over and over again to really believe someone cares for us.

When Sr. Ily taught me this method of prayer, it awakened in me a new level of understanding God's love. I did not know Scripture could "read" me or my life the way it did. I understood for the first time why Scripture was called the living word, as if it drew breath or was alive. Before learning this method of praying Scripture, I had found Bible readings lifeless, repetitive, vague, and unclear. Sr. Ily opened a door to the sacred for me. She taught me a practice that helped me grow in my desire for God and in my awareness of God's desire for me.

To this day, the prayer method of Lectio Divina is one of the main tools in my prayer toolbox. Like the other methods of prayer we have talked about already, this is another tool that supports my intentional prayer time with God and can occur within the walls of my home and within the silence of my own heart. I still use this tool—more than a decade after learning it—in a life that is much busier than it was when I took that busy-person's retreat at age twenty-one.

Scripture can be picked up and prayed anywhere and in any season of life. Why don't you give it a try?

Learning God's Voice

People ask me all the time, "How do I know if I'm hearing God's voice or not?" While I don't have the million-dollar answer to this question, I *can* tell you this: A way to recognize God's voice is to spend time praying with Scripture. Scripture is truly the word of God and voice of God. If we want to tune our ear to God's voice, why not start with what we know is God's word?

Think about it this way. In a room of young children, I distinctly know when one of my own children is calling out, "Mom!" or when it's another child. Why? Because I've spent hours and hours and hours listening to my children's voices. My ear is finely attuned to what their voices sound like. I can also typically discern which of my children is calling me. I do not think about this anymore; it's just something that naturally happens in motherhood—training our ear to our children's voices.

In the same way, as we continue to meditate on God's word, we become more and more attuned to what God's voice sounds like to us. This isn't foolproof by any means, and that's why St. Ignatius additionally offers us many suggestions for discernment (which we will talk about in a later chapter) to help us distinguish between God's voice and our own.

A Deepening Awareness

When Chris and I got married, right out of college, I was convinced that I knew everything about him and he knew everything about me. But daily living with each other and getting to know each other's idiosyncrasies ushered us into a whole new level of trust and love.

Our biggest disagreements in our first year of marriage were over the ways we did things in the kitchen. Both of our families are South Louisiana families that enjoy cooking, and one of our cherished wedding gifts was our very own cast-iron skillet used to make some of our culture's most popular dishes. Now, there are two schools of thought about how to care for a cast-iron skillet. One school insists on using no soap at all—just wipe it down, rinse it out, and let it dry on low heat on the stove. Chris's family falls into this school. The other school of thought recommends washing the skillet lightly with soap, rinsing it out, and letting it dry with the help of a stove. My family belongs to this one.

One night, after browning meat and making spaghetti in our cast-iron skillet, I soaped, washed, and rinsed our skillet. Needless to say, dear hubs was none too happy! This led to one of the biggest fights in our first year of marriage, that really had more to do with the merging of two lives than with the skillet itself. Even after all the time we had spent together in college and in marriage up to that point, there was still more to learn about each other—even down to our preferred way to clean a skillet.

It was not just in our early years of marriage that we came to know more about our love for each other. I can think of moments throughout our marriage that drew me into a whole new level of trust, vulnerability, and understanding of Chris's love for me and my love for him—like the time after our son, Brady, was born, when, because of the epidural's effects, I could not stand up by myself to go to the bathroom. With the gentleness that only a hubby can give, Chris helped me stand, escorted me to the bathroom, and kept a firm grasp on my arm the entire time so I would not fall. In a moment when I felt helpless, tired, weak, and incapable of taking care of my basic needs, Chris showed me dignity and love.

Or there are the ways we have learned to lean on each other during the last seven years of our marriage, when we did not have family nearby to support us. At another point, we needed to learn a new level of love and trust when Chris's job required him to travel and we experienced periods of being apart. What sustained us during those times was the history of our relationship and the trust and love we had already developed. We are continually surprised at how this love and understanding keep growing.

God, too, is always drawing us deeper in our relationship and in our understanding of God's love for us. Even when we may think we fully understand all this, God surprises us with a new revelation. It takes time to get to know God, to trust God, and to know God's love for us, just as it takes time to get to know friends or significant others, to trust and to know their love and care for us and our love and care for them. It takes time for us to be willing to open up to God. It amazes me how much more I still have to learn about God's love for me, all these years after my journey with God began!

Just as Chris and I grew in understanding of our love for each other, my understanding of God's love grew also. I went through the infatuation stage with God, where I thought I knew everything about God and that God knew everything about me. Yet I had more to learn about God loving me even when I felt weak, broken, and sinful. God's dignity and love for me held steady and strong in those moments. Life has dealt me its fair share of ups and downs, where the solid footing of my life felt flipped upside down, but the one constant through all the transitions, moves, and losses has been God's steadfast love.

Now, humbled by life, I know that I have only scratched the surface of my understanding of God's love for me. There is much more to learn. So what do I do? I keep showing up to be with God. I keep coming to prayer and letting God continue to surprise me as God reveals steadfast love to me time and time again.

Prayer Is the Key

Prayer is what opened me to an inkling that God saw me differently. It's what gave me the impression that God saw something more, something else. Ultimately, God saw me—all of me—and God somehow loved me, in spite of what God saw.

That was a freeing realization and a gift. God loves me as I am, whether I am cranky, angry, mad, full of joy, peaceful, or patient. This is the same awakening that I witness over and over again in spiritual direction—people understanding that God sees them differently than they think God does and that God loves them *as they are*. Every time I witness it, I say to God, "Pinch me! How do I get to watch your love grow in another person so closely?" It's a place for me that solidifies my belief that God is present and alive in our world today.

How do we awaken to God's infinite love for us? The answer is the same as before: Spend time with God! Tools such as Lectio Divina, the Examen, or the prayer of consideration support us in this showing up to be with God. When we spend time with God on a day-to-day basis, we grow in our love for God and in our understanding of God's love for us, just as we grow in our understanding of our love for another or another's love for us—by spending time together.

It took me a tremendous amount of time to trust God—to trust that I would not be hurt, to trust that God's love was freely given, and to understand the depth and steadfastness of God's love for me. It was hard for me to accept that receiving God's love did not require me to jump through hoops or meet certain standards to receive it or earn it. Being loved the way God loves us is counter to most human relationships in our lives, so I struggled to accept that to be loved by God, I simply had to be me, the person I currently was. There was not some line I had to cross before God wanted to be in relationship with me. God wanted a relationship with me now, as I was, not as who I was not.

Again, I did not come to this understanding of God's love for me overnight. It took time for me not only to build trust in God but also to understand the free gift of God's love for me. Why did it take so long? Who knows, really? Like all of us, I had my fair share of brokenness and wounds. (And I still do.) I had voices in my life that were telling me I was not good enough, and it felt easier to believe them than to believe God's voice telling me I was worthy of love. (It still is sometimes.) I would like to say I have this struggle nipped in the bud, once and for all, and that I never struggle to believe that I am worthy of God's love anymore. If I ever tell you that, know that I am lying!

What I know from my own experience and my ministry of spiritual direction is that God's unshakable love for us is one of the most difficult realities to accept. As one woman shared with me, "It's easier for me to believe in transubstantiation or in the Trinity than it is for me to believe that I am worthy of God's love."

But what I will tell you is this: It gets easier and easier to believe that we are worthy of God's love. After spending a great deal of time with God in prayer, I understand what Margaret Silf means when she says there is "a kind of knowing—the kind of knowing that afterward you can never not know."[10] One thing I now know and can no longer not know is the depth to which I am loved by God. Do I forget it at times? Yes! Do I need to be re-reminded of it? You bet! Do I try to inhibit my own understanding of this by making choices that do not honor the person I am before God or by listening to another person's

---

10. Margaret Silf, *The Other Side of Chaos* (Chicago: Loyola Press, 2011), 73.

voice instead of God's loving, merciful voice? Of course! Continually meeting God for prayer in the inner chapel makes it easier and easier to believe it, remember it, and live it.

I count God's love for us as the foundation of our faith. It's hard to look at our sinfulness without the lens of love. It's hard to know how to bring our faith into our daily life without knowing how much God loves us, because it is so easy—so darn easy—to forget this simple fact. It's hard to believe that God will walk with us in our suffering or help us make decisions if we do not believe God loves us, if we do not believe that God has plans for our welfare and not for our woe, if we do not believe that God created the world, including our very selves, and it is good. It is hard to have hope and joy if we do not know deep in our bones that we are loved by God.

If you are looking for a solid place to build your life, build it on God's love. If there is any message I want to impress upon you, it's this one: You are a beloved child of God. You are worthy of God's love *now*. You are good. You are created in God's image. You, too, are holy.

A Look at Your Life Now

- Who helped you know you were lovable? Who helped you learn to love?

- How do you feel about God's love for you? Do you question it? Do you feel unworthy of God's love? unsure? thankful? Are you wanting to grow in your understanding of it?

- How are you experiencing God's love right now? Through whom and what?

Sometime this week, pray Psalm 139 using the prayer method Lectio Divina.

6

Re-situate Your Life

At the ripe old age of twenty-nine, twelve years into my relationship with God, God surprised the heck out of me. Looking back now on this period of my life, I'm not sure if I thought God couldn't take me any deeper or if I thought my work in prayer was done, but God brought me to a deeper level of healing than I had ever experienced. Through this healing, God restored and transformed my brokenness and gave me a profound experience of divine mercy.

In 2008, Chris and I moved away from Baton Rouge, which was the only home I had known for twenty-eight years. Leaving home was one of the hardest things I ever did. Our entire life was uprooted and transplanted to Athens, Georgia, so that Chris could go to graduate school. I was excited for the journey ahead of us, and I knew it was the right step for our family, but I grieved the loss of our home, our extended families, our friends, and my ministry community. I felt as if someone had pulled a rug out from under me, and I could not regain my footing.

During our first year in Georgia, I did my best to rebuild a life that made sense. I tried to put things in order, get us settled into a home, make new friends, and get involved in our parish. Our family grew in that first year with the birth of our second child, Abby. The transition of the move combined with the arrival of a new child without the comfort and support of home and family made for a difficult time. Chris and I were adjusting to a new way of being in our marriage, just the two of us, without a large community of family and friends to surround us. We also experienced a transition in the rhythm of our life, as Chris's schedule changed every semester and we were piecing together income on top of his fellowship to make ends meet. My ministry work was almost nonexistent that first year, and I struggled to find work to do in my profession in such a small town that had a very small Catholic population.

This was yet another season in which everything that had ever made sense to me changed or was lost. The place we called home for twenty-eight years was six hundred miles away. We were on our own, without the large community of support we'd always had. Being part of that community had made us feel valued and worthwhile, like we belonged somewhere; now we felt alone and isolated, like we didn't belong. There were limited friendships that first year, and I faced many days alone with our toddler son and a newborn. Those early stages of motherhood can create isolation and loneliness at any point, but the dearth of relationships within this new city that first year was devastating. I felt alone, afraid, isolated, and desperate.

Even with the movement in my faith journey that I'd sustained up to that point, I came to realize during this season that I still tied some of my worth to my work and ministry. Prayer had opened me to a new identity in God, but this upheaval in my life made me question everything all over again. As I write about this, tears well up as I remember the loneliness and worthlessness I felt.

Events such as these bring us to our knees. They challenge everything we ever held as true and leave us grappling for something solid—anything or anyone to give us direction, a sense of purpose, and value. Such events, though, also open us up to God's mercy. They provide the opening for God to swoop in and transform all the darkness, hurt, and pain.

The many hours I spent alone in the house with a toddler and an infant left me with a lot of time to talk to God. My prayer life that year looked like a roller coaster, ebbing from the dark valleys of desperation, where my prayers echoed the cries of the psalmist, "My God, my God, why have you forsaken me?" (Ps. 22:1) to the mountain-peak songs of praise: "I will sing praises to my God all my life long" (Ps. 146:2). I think most of us hit a point like this sooner or later— or, if you're like me, you can name multiple times when life threw you such a curveball or you were faced with such challenge or pain that you could do nothing but simply cry out to God.

I judged my prayer constantly that year. I felt that I was not growing at all. I struggled to feel God's presence and was so desperate to feel it. I'm not sure if it was my desperation or the lingering desire I'd held for years to stop merely studying St. Ignatius and actually experience his Spiritual Exercises, but on July 6, 2009, with a four-week-old in my arms, I began the journey of making the Spiritual Exercises. I started the nine-month journey with a year of loss behind me that had stripped down everything I'd known and left me feeling bruised and worn from the transition.

The Woo of God's Mercy

The first few weeks of the Spiritual Exercises process were focused on God's love. These weeks of the process reminded me of my identity in God, of God's growing and infinite love for me, and of all the ways God had previously awakened me to God's love and was continuing to do so. Then I moved into what's called "the first week of the Exercises," in which I shifted to praying about things that get in the way of our growth in God and also praying for God's mercy.

During the early hours of one of those September mornings, I had a life-changing moment in prayer that eventually led me to a whole new experience of God's mercy. As I sat with the day's Scripture, three words kept surfacing in my heart and mind: *Resituate your life.*

My initial reaction went something like this: *Resituate my life? Are you kidding me? Isn't that what we just did this past year? You cannot be asking me to do this again, God. I cannot handle it! I am broken, tired, and exhausted from this resituating of my life.*

God was not inviting me to move back home or to move somewhere else. Instead, God was inviting me to center my life fully around God and not around the other things that appeared good. Because, let's be clear: family, creating a home, feeling settled, and our work are all good things. The issue that catches us is when these things take center stage and we try to align the rest of our lives around them instead of God.

For me, the first year of living in Athens was an attempt to center our new life around our family, settling in, and finding meaningful work. The result left me feeling tired, alone, exhausted, aimless, and extremely restless. What started out as a move across the country spiraled as I tried to figure it out all on my own. I desperately needed help in healing my hurts and receiving forgiveness for attempting to center my life around anything other than God.

But God, out of abundant loving-kindness for me, would not let me remain broken, bruised, exhausted, and tired. God refused to leave me there. See, all those hours and hours of prayer that felt so hard in that first year had accomplished something without my noticing it. They made me turn to God in a way I never had before. Without realizing it, I was learning to trust God and lean on God. Those bumpy moments of prayer nurtured my relationship with God in such a way that I began to realize all over again the depths to which God loved me. God loved me enough to be willing to transform the dark aspects of my life. God let me feel sorrow for my choices and seek to do better with God's help.

This was an experience of God's mercy.

You see, someone who loves you is not going to let you sit in darkness, hurting and in pain. That person is going to come after you and sit with you and help you through whatever is going on. This is exactly what God did for me. God hunted the darkness—those parts I tried to hide from God and from other people, including my husband. But as the light of God's love grew within me, it began to shine on the dark areas, one of which was the truth that I was not situated fully in God's presence. Yes, I was a woman of prayer. In fact, I was a woman in ministry. But many pieces of my life that year were more centered on family, on creating a sense of home, and on work. I was actually staking my contentment on those things. Thus, my life was like a lopsided bike wheel, with multiple hubs and spokes going every which way. It just didn't work.

I knew the invitation was loud and clear. It rang out over and over again during my prayer: *Resituate your life. Resituate your life. Resituate your life.* God's invitation was to orient all my life around this foundational relationship of love and to let the rest of my life flow out of that relationship.

When it came down to it, I learned that I had been hiding quite a lot of my pain and hurt from God, thinking it was not of God's concern or interest. I know I am not alone in this. I watch this happen in spiritual direction; a person attempts to keep a piece of him- or herself—often it's brokenness—away from God. Who knows why we do this, really? The reason probably falls somewhere between our believing there is no way God can restore what is broken and our believing that what we did or experienced is so bad that we are unworthy of God's gift of redemption.

In that moment, I was holding a bit of both. Part of me didn't want to bring my loneliness, loss, and hurt to God because I didn't think it mattered or could be restored. The other part of me thought I had messed up so badly that God could not possibly forgive me.

But, surprise! Not only did God show me that I was loved and not alone through all of it, but also God showed me that my hurts, brokenness, and sinfulness mattered. And more than that, God could do the impossible and restore what I thought would never be whole again. This did not happen overnight, by any means, but rather through my showing up in prayer and bringing all my life before God—even the yucky, dark realities of my life.

It felt impossible at first. I had no idea how to orient my entire life, especially the negatives, around God. God did not give up on me, though. Nor will God give up on you. Whatever you are holding back, whatever your struggles are, whatever choices you've made that you're not proud of, whatever hurt that was caused by someone else—God cares about it. Bring it before God, and ask God for forgiveness and healing. And God will not stop shining love and light on your brokenness until you are restored and healed.

This is what mercy is about: God not giving up on us. God not abandoning us. God doing the impossible. God restoring us when we think there is no way we can be restored. God coming after us, even when we are so broken and wounded that we think God has left. God changing and softening our hearts. God providing what we need when we are desperate. God forgiving what feels unforgivable.

Mercy's Light

God leaves nothing untried in reaching out to sinners,[11] which each of us is. Pope Francis describes God's mercy this way:

---

11. Andrea Tornielli, "Note to the Reader" in Pope Francis, *The Name of God Is Mercy* (New York: Random House, 2016), xix.

[God's mercy is] like the sky: we look at the sky when it is full of stars, but when the sun comes out in the morning, with all its light, we don't see the stars anymore. That is what God's mercy is like: a great light of love and tenderness because God forgives not with a decree, but with a caress. [He does it] by caressing the wounds of our sin because he is involved in forgiving, he is involved in our salvation.[12]

God's love is so bright and so strong that it simply refuses to allow darkness to stay in our hearts. God shines light upon these places and invites us not only to see them but also to bring them to God so that God can transform them.

God shone his light into how lonely I felt in Athens and not only walked with me in my loneliness but also brought beautiful friend-ships and a new community of support into our life. God shone his light on my choice to orient just some of my life, instead of all of it, around God, and God helped me make a better choice. As I brought one relationship after another, one hurt after another, and all of my life to God, I'm here to tell you, *healing happened.* Forgive-ness also happened, which enabled me to then forgive myself. I was relieved from feeling so alone and isolated. God healed me where it hurt the most.

Don't we all want this—to experience relief from our suffering? to be forgiven? to have our wounds tended? God is the one who can do this for us. Prayer provides the space for God to enter our hearts and transform them. In the interior chapel we carry, God's mercy abounds, and all God needs is a crack to let in love and light. The crack might be a moment that brings us to our knees, or it might simply be the inkling of the desire for healing. If we acknowledge our need for God, God comes in and offers mercy. God's gift of mercy changes us, transforms us, and makes us whole. Even when we are

---

12. Ibid., xvi.

broken, tired, and wounded, God enters this space and restores our spirits, strengthens us for the journey, heals us, and transforms us.

What Are Our Dark Realities?

While God's mercy is always offered to us, the reality is that we can close ourselves off from the gift of it. We are humans, which means we are sinners. We make choices that lead us away from God—choices like mine that kept God from being at the center of every aspect of my life.

Here are a few possible dark places in our lives:

We stop showing up.

When we do this, we stop acknowledging our relationship with God, or we stop spending time with God. We completely turn away. We stop showing up for all sorts of reasons, even though God is waiting on us and will never grow tired of waiting on us.

We hide parts of our lives.

We bring most of our life before God but try to hide our deepest hurts and wounds or our choices and actions we are not proud of; we are too afraid to bring them into the light.

We harden our hearts.

The reality is, life can sometimes harden our hearts. Loss, transition, and pain can make us brace ourselves, closing our hearts so that we don't get hurt again. When we do this, we can keep God from entering our hearts also.

We do not forgive.

Harboring anger, hurt, or bitterness prevents God's life from flourishing in us. Our braced stance gives the impression that we believe God cannot do the impossible. This is why Jesus invites us to forgive

not just once but over and over again—"seventy-seven times"
(Matt. 18:21–22). We do not forgive alone; it is God who helps us
forgive. So often, though, we hold on to our hurts and our grudges;
instead of harboring love, we harbor the poison of resentment.

We are hurt or suffering.

We experience hurt or we suffer, and out of our natural humanness,
we close up and seek to protect ourselves. The hurt might be caused
by others, by life circumstances, or even by our own actions or
responses. It is our choice to let God into this experience or not.

We are closed to the newness of God.

We close our hearts off to the newness God is trying to birth within
us. Another way to say it is, we're afraid of change. We are scared or
fearful of what God might be doing in us, and we run the other direction or close our hearts to the possibility of rebirth or new birth.

We cling to the world's values.

Our priorities do not align with the values of the Gospel. Perhaps we
place value on getting ahead at any cost, on earning our worth, and
on striving for power not congruent with the values of our faith.

We make choices that do not align with God's desires for us.

Even though we know what is right or what God is asking us to do,
we make a different choice. Often upon doing so we feel remorse or
restlessness due to the misalignment of our action with God's desires.

You might be wondering, *Why does it matter if I know the dark spots
of my life?* I sometimes wonder that myself, because it's not fun to
name our sins or dark spots. But if we do not name them and bring
them into our awareness, we cannot intentionally invite God to work
in these shadowy areas. The gift of God's mercy is available to each
of us, and as Pope Francis reminds us: "The medicine is there, the

healing is there, if only we take a small step toward God or even just desire to take that step."[13]

Naming Our Darkness and the Examen's Role

It's not easy to name or confront our brokenness or our sinfulness. It's hard to name our shortcomings and the deep wounds of heart. But I want to return to the Examen prayer here and describe how it can support us in this process of learning God's mercy.

We spoke of the Examen prayer in chapter 4. It's a method that builds our awareness of where we feel God's presence each day, but it also helps us notice where we struggle to feel God's presence and light. In the fourth step, we ask ourselves, *Where did I struggle to feel or name God's presence?*

It can be hard to examine each day, looking for what kept us from growing spiritually, but we have to learn to look at our actions, our words, and our thoughts with God's eyes. When the invitation to resituate my life was at the forefront of my prayer, the Examen was an invaluable tool that helped me understand what part of my life was off center. As I prayed the Examen daily, I began to notice recurring themes as I reached step four: the depth of my hurt from the loss of leaving home, the attempt to keep pieces of my life away from God, and the belief that I did not feel God could restore my brokenness.

In essence, I was naming my hurts and sins. This is a key piece of the journey of the Spiritual Exercises. And while not all of us will make the Spiritual Exercises, a piece of acknowledging the restlessness we sometimes feel is naming what keeps us from growing in God, and that often comes down to naming our sins.

When these pieces first came to my attention in prayer, it was hard to accept the depth of my hurt and the impact of the choice I had

---

13. Ibid., xviii.

made to give only part of my life to God. God brought this to my consciousness slowly over time, reminding me all the while of God's love for me. In the end, the Examen helped me say what was closing me off to the gift of God's mercy and ask for forgiveness.

The Examen is a tool that continues to guide me spiritually because it helps me see what's getting in the way of deepening my relationship with God. Once we name what it is in the fourth step, we make amends to do better in the fifth step, and we ask God for the grace we need to do so.

Praying the Colloquy

St. Ignatius offers us another way to notice and name the real center of life, and it is called the colloquy. In this prayer, we are invited to imagine ourselves at the foot of Jesus' cross and to pray with three questions:

1. What have I done for Christ?
2. What am I doing for Christ?
3. What ought I do for Christ?

When I prayed with these three questions during my time of making the Spiritual Exercises, I was able to see what choices and things I had done for Christ and what things I had done out of another motivation —maybe my own ego, my desire to be a people pleaser, or my fear of conflict. It allowed me to name the areas of my life that were already being lived out of my relationship with Christ, and I began to get clear on what specific task Christ was calling me to do. (We'll address this more in a later chapter.)

I turn to these questions many times in my prayer life. They give me clarity about what I am doing and not doing for God, and they help me know what I ought to be doing in the first place. What I have learned over the years of praying is that when I am living fully into what I ought to be doing for Christ, I feel at peace and much more alive than when I am continually choosing to act opposite of God's invitation for me.

God Does the Transforming Work

I invite you to consider using the three questions of the colloquy in your prayer. I also extend another invitation to try the Examen. Both the Examen and the colloquy offer us ways to bring our darkness to God in prayer so we can receive mercy.

And the great gift of God's relationship with us is that we do not have to face those dark spots or try to transform them on our own. God does the heavy lifting for us by helping us carry our burdens and by tending to the wounds of our heart. Naming our sinfulness is not just about being aware but also about letting God enter into those sins with us and transform them so we can go and "sin no more" (John 8:11).

I would be lying if I told you I never attempted to center my life around something other than God again. That's a part of our humanity. We make choices that lead us away from God. But what I can tell you is that the transformation that took place as God resituated my life fully around himself was life changing. My life came to feel that it was in the right order, and a deep peace came with that.

On the days I center my life around something or someone other than God, I quickly feel the restlessness rush in. The feeling that something is "off" is God's way of awakening me to my choices. With this awakening comes, again, God's gift of mercy and the invitation, yet again, to restore the orientation of my life and choices fully around God.

We Are Called to This

Sometimes when we build our awareness of the dark spots in our lives, we may ask ourselves, *Why would God want to be in a relationship with me, anyway?* I've asked myself this question a million times. *Why would God call me, a sinner, not only to be in relationship but also to do the ministry that I do?* I felt this big time after realizing that my life was not fully centered on God. I beat myself up a bit and questioned if God wanted to still use me for the ministry I do.

But the reality is, God calls us in spite of our sinfulness and brokenness.

God first and foremost calls us and invites us to relationship. Second, God calls us to be part of the work of God's kingdom right now, as we are. Need an example for evidence? Let's look at Peter. Peter was one of Jesus' closest friends, his chosen disciple. This is also the man Jesus predicted would deny him three times, which he did. Even though Peter would deny being a follower of Jesus not one, not two, but *three* times, Jesus said to him, "You are Peter, and on this rock I will build my church" (Matt. 16:18). Jesus handed his mission to a man who had turned his back on Jesus in his time of need. Why would Jesus do that?

The interaction in John's Gospel between Peter and Jesus is one of my favorites:

When they had finished breakfast, Jesus said to Simon Peter, "Simon son of John, do you love me more than these?" He said to him, "Yes, Lord; you know that I love you." Jesus said to him, "Feed my lambs." A second time he said to him, "Simon son of John, do you love me?" He said to him, "Yes, Lord; you know that I love you." Jesus said to him, "Tend my sheep." He said to him the third time, "Simon son of John, do you love me?" Peter felt hurt because he said to him the third time, "Do you love me?" And he said to him, "Lord, you know everything; you know that I love you." Jesus said to him, "Feed my sheep." (John 21:15–17)

This exchange between Jesus and Peter occurs after Peter's denial, and Jesus not only forgives Peter and offers Peter mercy but also gives him a task: Feed my sheep!

The same is true for us. God forgives us and offers us mercy, no matter what we have done. God's mercy makes the dark spots in our lives holy. It is this unearned, freely given gift of God's mercy that shows up in the middle of our busy lives and restores us. And then, like Peter, we, too, are given a task and are called to spread God's message of mercy because we know what it means to have received mercy in the first place. We know what it's like to be healed, restored, repaired, and forgiven. It is because of this gift of love and mercy, and out of this gift of love and mercy, that we are called to fully follow God's son, Jesus.

Let's turn now to what it looks like to follow Jesus in real life.

A Look at Your Life Now

- What keeps me from opening to the gift of God's mercy?
- Where am I experiencing, or where have I experienced, God's mercy?
- What are the dark aspects in my life that need God's transforming power?
- How am I experiencing being called by God despite my darkness?

Pray the colloquy, and then write down your responses to each question:

- What have I done for Christ?
- What am I doing for Christ?
- What ought I do for Christ?

7

Prayer within the Reality of Life

I'm not sure if you've noticed, but so far I have not spoken much about Jesus in this book. St. Ignatius, in his *Spiritual Exercises*, invites us to pray with God's love and God's mercy before inviting us to walk closely and intimately with the Person of Jesus. So that's what I've done in this book also. We have acknowledged our restlessness, learned how we can begin our prayer lives, and explored how we can deepen our understanding of God's love and God's mercy. Now I want us to turn to the process of encountering Jesus, the man who fully reveals God to us.

Who Is Jesus?

Who is this man Jesus, in whom we profess our faith and for whose arrival generations and generations waited? Jesus was a man from the royal line of King David, who was born in a village from which it was predicted the Messiah would come. His name was given to his mother in a dream; as a baby he was presented in a temple, and great things were envisioned of him. The brief glimpses of his youth we find in Scripture show a teenager spending his time with the wise temple teachers, and a teenager raised to reverence his faith. We see a man who had a profound experience of God in the desert and who came back from that experience charged with sharing a message of

God's love. Jesus taught us about God through his stories and actions. Some might view Jesus as a radical, a man who stood for love and compassion and who stood against what was the natural order of his time. Jesus was a man who had the courage to go to Jerusalem and face those who most threatened him—a man who, as he hung on the cross, cried out to God for help. Yet, while in agony there on the cross, he offered comfort to his mother and best friend, and he offered forgiveness to the man hanging on the cross next to him. Jesus was a man who promised us the great gift of the Holy Spirit so that he could continue to be God in us and with us.

Those are the facts of Jesus' life. Some of us have, since childhood, heard the stories that tell us about Jesus. There's a difference, though, in just hearing these stories and in letting these stories help us build a relationship with Jesus. Maybe we know of Jesus, but do we really know him intimately? In the Gospel of John, Jesus makes it pretty clear that to know God, one must know Jesus:

> Jesus said to [Thomas], "I am the way, and the truth, and the life. No one comes to the Father except through me. If you know me, you will know my Father also. From now on you do know him and have seen him." (John 14:6–7)

So, how do we get to know Jesus? One of the best ways I can offer you is to pray with the Gospels, because it is in these four books of the Bible that we encounter the Person of Jesus. We read of his actions. We hear his words. We see whom he loves and how he loves them. It is by praying with these Scriptures that we not only come to understand what Jesus teaches us about God, his Father, but also come to personally know Jesus.

Praying with the Gospels

In chapter 5, we talked about using the prayer method of Lectio Divina to pray with the Scriptures. This method of prayer works wonderfully with any of the books in the Bible, including the Gospels. We can pick any passage from the books of Matthew, Mark, Luke, or John and pray with it using the four steps of Lectio Divina: read, reflect, respond, rest. This way of praying with the life of Jesus allows us to fine-tune our ears and our heart to what Jesus is doing.

In this chapter I want to introduce you to a second way of praying with Scripture that St. Ignatius recommended; I think it's especially helpful when praying with the Gospels. It is called *Ignatian contemplation*. During this type of prayer, we are invited to use our imagination. Through the use of imagination, we notice what God is teaching us. Ignatian contemplation allows us to enter the events of Jesus' life and get to know him intimately.

How to Pray Using Ignatian Contemplation

Here are basic steps to this powerful form of prayer.

Select a Scripture.

Pick a passage from one of the four Gospels: Matthew, Mark, Luke, or John.

Read.

Read the passage several times slowly so that you almost know the story well enough to share it with another person.

Imagine the scene.

Close your eyes and imagine the scene. For instance, if you are praying with the scene of Jesus' birth in the manger, imagine what this scene looks like. Who is in the scene? What are they doing? Where are they located? What do you notice about the environment? What do you smell? What do you hear? Let the Holy Spirit guide this unfolding event in your mind.

Put yourself in the scene.

As the scene begins to take shape, put yourself in it. Notice where you end up. Again, with Jesus' birth in the manger, notice: *Am I standing by Mary or Joseph? Am I peering into the manger to sneak a peek at baby Jesus? Am I off at a distance as an observer? Am I standing by the animals?*

Notice what happens.

Let the story unfold in your mind. Stay with the Scripture story in prayer.

Respond and rest.

Share with God what you noticed and experienced. Then rest in God and let God speak to you.

Reflect.

Reflect on what you experienced during this prayer. What did you learn about Jesus? About God? About another character in the story? About yourself?

To give you an example of this practice from my own prayer, I'll use this passage of Jesus' birth. I prayed this story when our daughter Abby was six months old. As I closed my eyes and let the scene play out in my life, I noticed that I was standing next to Mary. My own heart that was bursting with pride at my newborn child matched the way Mary lovingly stared at her son, Jesus. I watched as Mary tended to Jesus, nursed him, clothed him, and rocked him. I realized that Mary was doing the same actions I did with Abby every day.

It was through this prayer that God showed me the humanity of Jesus and Mary. It was the first time I experienced Mary in her human motherness, not only as the revered mother of God. She showed Jesus love through the concrete acts of caring for his basic needs, the same as I do for my own children. Through this perspective, I suddenly understood what it meant that Jesus *fully* entered our humanity and what it meant that Jesus came to this world as an infant, relying on another's care.

We can pray with all the events of Jesus' life using this method of Ignatian contemplation. We can turn to his presentation at the temple or when his parents lost track of him when he was twelve. We can pray with his time in the desert and the many events in his public ministry. We can also pray with his Passion and resurrection. Each of these stories of Jesus' life teaches us something about God. Jesus fully reveals God to us. Yes, Jesus is both human and divine. But it is the person of Jesus, the human person, who teaches us about God.

What Does Jesus Teach Us about God?

If we want to know about God's characteristics—what is God like?—then the most direct way to answer that question is to look at Jesus.

Jesus teaches us whom God loves.

First, we learn who God loves: everyone. Jesus makes it clear that all people are loved, even the people society deems not worthy of God's love. In Jesus' time, the "unworthy" were tax collectors, prostitutes, lepers, the blind, and the poor. Jesus stops and encounters the people on his path—the blind men, the woman about to be stoned, the woman who suffered an ongoing hemorrhage. He has relationships with people we might feel do not make the cut, just as the Pharisees and scribes thought. Jesus called as his closest friends a crew made up of men who were fishermen and tax collectors. We also see Jesus loving and caring for his family—his mother, Mary; his father, Joseph; his cousin, John the Baptist. He reclined at table with sinners, prostitutes, and the poorest of the poor. Jesus shows us that God's love is not just for people like the Pharisees or scribes, who were elders in the Jewish faith—today's "Pharisees" might be our own religious leaders or other people with a lot of clout. God's love reaches out to all people, including each one of us.

Jesus teaches us how God loves.

Through concrete action, Jesus shows us how God loves. In the Gospels we see Jesus showing us how God loves through healing, forgiveness, mercy, and compassion. Jesus sees and responds to the deepest needs of human hearts. To a blind person he gives sight; to a paralyzed person he gives the ability to stand up and walk; to a leper and social outcast he gives cleansing and restoration to community; to a woman isolated by her illness he gives healing in both body and soul; to a person with a sinful history he gives mercy and hope for a better future.

Jesus shows us how God looks at us with eyes of compassion and love, accepting us where we are and loving us as we are. Jesus doesn't wait for people to be perfect or have their lives in order or for them to sin no more. Rather, Jesus enters the messiness of humanity and encounters people along the way in their brokenness, hurt, and mess.

Jesus shows us how God acts.

Through all the ways Jesus concretely models for us the way God loves, he also shows us how God acts. Jesus demonstrates that God does not tire of waiting for us—that we are not abandoned. Jesus shows us that God will go to any extreme to draw us into relationship with him and will go to any extreme to offer the gift of mercy and love. It's up to us to receive it or refuse it. God acts out of love and mercy, and Jesus shows us this. God goes beyond the law to offer mercy and compassion; Jesus shows us this, for instance, when he heals on the Sabbath. God will forgive and heal what is broken within us, and Jesus models this type of healing. Jesus also shows us that there are consequences to our actions and that we have a role in accepting the gift of relationship with God. He shows us that, sadly, there are some who turn away with hardened hearts and some who simply cannot follow Jesus, such as the rich young man who could not leave his possessions behind.

Jesus Models the Way

Jesus teaches us many things about God. Jesus also models the way for us to live: rooted in God and living in the reality of this divine-and-human life. To illustrate this, let me use an example I came across years ago in Margaret Silf's book *Companions of Christ*.[14] It's the image of the oil lamp. Since coming across her initial writing about the oil lamp, I have incorporated and expanded on it throughout my retreat work. Let's take a closer look at this example.

The oil lamp represents us. In each of us, there is a "wick" that runs through us. One end of this wick is immersed in the oil, and the other end of the wick is extended outward, hoping to bring light. We are like this oil lamp in that we can choose to root our lives somewhere—be it God or anyone or anything else. Where we immerse the wick affects what we bring out into the world. This is how most of us live; we attempt to ground our lives somewhere or in someone, and we live in the world, just as Jesus did.

Jesus demonstrates that if we root our lives in God, we can live in the world, bringing light and hope to all we encounter, and we can walk through anything that comes our way. If our oil is God, we never run out of it. Our wick is always fed and fueled and is capable of lighting.

---

14. Margaret Silf, *Companions of Christ* (Grand Rapids, MI: Eerdmans, 2005), 94.

But let's be honest. Sometimes, we pull our wick out of the "oil of God," and we place it instead in the oil of our work or of our pursuit of money or ambition. Perhaps we center our lives and ground our lives in family or in another person, hoping that that person can continually refuel and provide the oil we need to live in the world. Maybe our other end of the wick can give light for a while, but eventually we realize that our light is flickering and fading and not giving much help to anyone.

And then there are times when we're not grounded in anything. Our wick is not immersed in any kind of oil. We feel empty, restless, longing for meaning. Imagine trying to light an oil lamp without any oil. We can try multiple times to light it, but without oil, nothing happens.

Jesus shows us how to keep our oil lamp fueled and lit. Jesus shows us how to live in the world and how to live a life of prayer while tending to our roles and responsibilities. Jesus was not a hermit, focusing his entire day on prayer with God. He was out there in the world, as each of us is. He was in relationships. He was doing his work. He encountered people of all kinds, just as we do each day.

Now let's take a closer look at each end of the wick.

The Wick in the Oil

What will keep our wick in the oil? If we turn to Jesus, we see a clear example of what kept Jesus' wick in the oil—that is, how he kept his connection with his heavenly Father. He prayed. It's that simple. Jesus took time to be with his Father.

Once, out of curiosity about Jesus' prayer life, I flipped through the Gospels to find examples of Jesus praying. It didn't take long to come up with this list of recorded moments of Jesus praying:

> Matthew 6:9–13 Jesus teaches us how to pray.
> Matthew 11:25–26 Jesus praises God.

Matthew 14:23 Jesus withdraws to pray in the evening.

Mark 1:35 Jesus finds a deserted place to pray in the morning.

Luke 4:42 Jesus prays even though people need him.

Luke 5:16 Jesus makes time for prayer within his work.

Luke 6:12 Jesus withdraws to pray for a night.

Luke 22:32 Jesus prays for his friend.

Luke 22:41–44 Jesus begs God for help.

Luke 23:34 Jesus asks God to forgive.

John 11:41–42 Jesus thanks God for hearing his prayer.

John 17:1–26 Jesus prays for us.

If we look at this list, which is by no means exhaustive, what do we notice about Jesus' prayer life? Jesus prayed at all times of day—in the morning and at night and throughout the day. We see that Jesus stopped his prayer to tend to the needs of people and his work. We see Jesus praising and thanking God, begging God for help, and asking God to forgive. We see Jesus praying for other people: those he healed and taught, his friends, and us. We also see Jesus teaching *us* to pray by giving us the Our Father prayer.

What does this mean for us? It shows us the value of prayer and the ways we can incorporate prayer into daily life. Jesus lets us know that it is time spent with God that enables him and empowers him to do what he does. Prayer keeps our wick immersed in this resource we call God's presence.

Community

Looking to Jesus as a model for how to live, we also notice the importance of community. Jesus grew up in the Jewish tradition and honored the Jewish rituals and practices: weddings, the Sabbath, participation at the Temple, and special holy days such as Passover. I think this speaks to us about the value of faith communities in our own lives. Jesus not only surrounded himself with a community of friends, but he also practiced his Jewish faith.

Jesus' model shows me, a practicing Catholic, that one way I keep my wick in the oil is my participation in the faith community. Jesus' example shows me that there is value in attending Sunday Mass, which is, in itself, modeled on one of Jesus' actions, the Last Supper. While Jesus did not have the sacraments as we do, the rituals and special moments of the Jewish faith in which he engaged were not just meaningless habits but moments that made holy encounter possible. Today's Christian sacraments open us to receive new graces and gifts from God that further us on our journey.

For instance, Jesus was baptized by John the Baptist. When this happened, the sky opened and a dove descended over Jesus' head, and a voice was heard saying, "You are my Son, in whom I am well pleased." The sacrament of baptism in the Catholic faith is a major milestone on our faith journey, opening us to receive the gifts of our baptism: freedom from original sin, welcome into our Christian community, and entrance into the broader global faith community.

Jesus shows us that community plays a unique role in helping us keep our wick in the oil, so to speak. We do not have to go at it alone. We can lean on the wisdom of a community of believers to walk the road together, learning from and with one another. A faith community, like my Catholic parish, plays a vital role in keeping my life fueled and ready to give light to the world.

Relationships

Beyond a community, Jesus also had friends. He surrounded himself with twelve disciples. He was friends with people such as Mary and Martha. We see him weeping when he learns of his friend Lazarus's death. He had a close relationship with his cousin John the Baptist. Jesus is the Son of God, both human and divine, yet he took the time to make close relationships. He leaned on his friends, the disciples, to spread his mission and be part of his work. He both gave to and received from them. He begged them to keep watch with him. He opened his heart to his friends, and his friends opened their hearts to him.

What this tells me is that friendships and close relationships with people of similar values are a crucial part of our faith journey. These are friends who will pray with you, attend faith services with you, and celebrate sacraments and moments of ritual with you. They will recline at table with you but will also be with you in your trials. Even though the disciples fell short of being with Jesus through his crucifixion, Jesus still loved them and called them friends.

What about us? Do we have friendships like this—people who are heart friends and help us walk this path of faith? I am thankful for the women and men God has put in my life to help me on my journey. Some of these friendships come and go, and some are still part of my life, encouraging me and always walking with me to a deeper place with God. These men and women encourage me to keep my "wick in the oil" and not center my life elsewhere. They wake me up when I am attempting to go down a path that is not right for me. If you cannot name friends like this, stop now and ask God for friendships to support you on your faith journey.

We don't have to go at it alone. We not only have God, but we also can have a community of people to stand with us as we seek to ground our lives in God.

The Extended End of the Wick

Let's turn now to the other end of our wick, the end that is extended fully out into the world. The majority of us are not called to live in monasteries or convents or to be hermits. There are beautiful men and women called to a cloistered life of prayer, but the world is made up primarily of men and women who are called to the vocation of being laypeople, whether they are single, married, or widowed.

For those of us who are laypersons, our vocations and our prayer lives happen within the world, not apart from it. Our prayer life feeds the rest of our life. And once again, Jesus is an example of this type of lived vocation. He was not living a cloistered life, dedicated solely to prayer. Jesus had his feet on the ground—literally. He was walking the streets, encountering people of all kinds. He was part of the world, not separate from it. And it was within this reality—the loud, chaotic, busy reality of life—that Jesus ministered to and served others.

We, like Jesus, are called to a life of prayer that happens within our roles and responsibilities. We, like Jesus, are called to be in the world, not separate from it, and it is within our living in the world that we are called to bring the light of God to others. St. Ignatius names this being a *contemplative in action*, which simply means that we are people of prayer who are called to live an active life out in the world.

Sometimes we think that living out a Christian vocation means being a missionary in a foreign land or working at a church. Let's be clear: some people are called to this lifestyle, and that's a vocation given to them by God. But if someone is a teacher or nurse or lawyer or accountant or businessperson or social worker, does this mean that he or she is not living out a vocation? No! If you look to the saints, you find people with charisms and gifts for all kinds of vocations—saints who are called to be evangelizers like St. Paul, or saints who are called to work with the poor like St. Teresa of Calcutta. St. Xavier, one of St. Ignatius's closest companions, had a passion for foreign mission work. Each of these saints used the gifts God gave them to live out their vocations. These are all great and holy calls, but as St. Teresa adequately reminds us, "If you want world peace, go home and love your family."

Where we live out our faith life starts with the people we encounter daily. This is where we are called to bring our light into the world, as Jesus did. How do we know where this might be? Let's start by looking at four questions.

1. Who has God given us to love? The first four names on my list are going to be my husband and three children. My list is going to expand then to extended family and friends—the people God places in my life to be in close relationship with. My prayer life and the time I spend with God influence the love and light I can bring to my loved ones. And my loved ones can tell when my prayer life is off! I get snippy, cranky, and lack energy for the basic tasks when this happens. My time with God is vital to my ability to be in relationship with the loved ones in my life.

2. Who is my neighbor? My neighbor is the one I tangibly encounter in any given day. This means that part of our call is to bring our faith into the interactions we have with each person we encounter. This doesn't mean preaching the Gospel to every person using words, but it means loving people the way Jesus did—with dignity and respect. It means looking at others with the compassionate eyes of God. And how do we put on the lens of God's compassionate gaze? You've probably guessed it by now: We spend time with God in prayer, just as Jesus did! Jesus, through the time he spent with his Father, learned to love as God loves. The same is true for us.

3. What is our work? Our work may or may not involve an official ministry role. Jesus shows us that we can go about our jobs and fully use the gifts God gave us. Our invitation, though, is to center our lives in God through prayer and then let our time with God feed our work, our decisions, and our choices. What would it look like for you to be a man or woman of prayer in your work life? If God were guiding your choices and actions, how might your work decisions change? Again, this is where we spend the majority of our weeks—at work. Can you imagine not letting your relationship with God affect where you spend the bulk of your time?

4. What are our other responsibilities? Our list of other responsibilities may encompass civic and community duties, volunteer organizations, and church or school activities. These have their proper places. And we can allow our growing relationship with God to influence the way we function in these situations.

Jesus showed us the way to live. We can extend our wick out into the world and let God open us to God's love and mercy, and as we do this, it allows us to bring a bit of what we received from God in prayer to the people we encounter in work and home life, in all we are called to do. This is how we live as disciples of Jesus.

The Cost of Discipleship

I frequently question my call to discipleship. It's easy for me to make a list a mile long of the reasons I am not qualified to be one of Jesus' disciples or to show that I am not cut out for the task Jesus invites me to do. I might question my ability to love my spouse or raise our children the way God asks me to. I often doubt my abilities as a woman in her thirties serving in the roles of retreat facilitator, writer, and spiritual director. I look at my shortcomings and faults and think there is no way in the world God would invite me to do the ministry God has invited me to do. There are a million more people holier than I am, and there must be someone else who does not make mistakes like I do. I ask, *Why me, Lord? Why would you choose me?*

But here's the deal: Jesus calls us now, as we are. Jesus is not waiting for us to be completely healed or whole or to reach some point in our faith journey that magically qualifies us for discipleship. No, Jesus calls us now. Right now. We are invited into a relationship with Jesus.

We are invited to be part of Jesus' work on this earth. This means starting today. And how do we do that? We pray. We bring our lives before God, and we go about living the life God gave us to live.

There is a cost, though, to discipleship. The cost of discipleship is transformation. Encountering Jesus in prayer will change you. I tell people all the time that if you like your life exactly as it is and do not want to change and you like your relationships exactly as they are, then do *not* start praying. Because when you begin a life of prayer and you encounter Jesus, he will invite you to make changes. I'm not sharing this to scare you away from prayer but to share with you the reality of what happens.

Following Jesus transforms your life. And let's be honest—sometimes we don't want our lives transformed or altered in any way. (Or maybe that's just me!) But when I look back on my relationship with Jesus, I see a journey full of gifts and surprises. I met people, and still meet people, I never would have met otherwise but who became heart friends because of Jesus. I experience unconditional love, constant companionship, healing, forgiveness, and mercy because of Jesus. Being in a relationship with Jesus stretches me to love in places or ways I never thought I could. I've been healed in places that felt incapable of being healed and restored in places that seemed irreparable because Jesus is part of my life. In addition, Jesus helped me forgive others in situations I thought were impossible and to love people I thought I had been too hurt by to love anymore. Jesus expanded my eyes to see the world beyond the four walls of my home and to see the need for mercy in this world.

Being loved by Jesus called me outward, and still does, to put this love into action. I did things I never dreamed of doing because I allowed Jesus to enter my life: becoming a spiritual director in my thirties, leading Ignatian retreats, and writing on prayer and spirituality. What I do with my days and nights looks different from what I ever dreamed would be true at this stage of my life. I did not set out to do any of these things, and trust me when I say that I doubted (and still doubt at times) that I could do any of the things Jesus invited me to do. Yet every time I doubted or was afraid or felt a lack of confidence, Jesus, through his accompanying presence, provided the strength I needed, the grace I needed, and the courage I needed to take a step forward. He still provides this for me today.

Friendship with Jesus will change you. It's a radical transformation, really, one that we might be afraid to let happen. One that we might do everything we can to fight. But trust me: Even with the shifts and tweaks that a relationship with Jesus brings into your life, it is worth it. The gift of a relationship with Jesus brings abundant joy and peace and an accompanying presence, no matter what life throws at you—and it is to these unexpected turns in life and how prayer helps us walk through them that we turn next.

A Look at Your Life Now

- What and who will help me keep my "wick in the oil"?
- To whom and to what situations am I called to bring the light of Christ?
- How do I experience the cost of discipleship?

Choose a Scripture from one of the Gospels. Pray this Scripture using the prayer method of Ignatian contemplation.

8

Through Tough Spots

When my son, Brady, was almost three years old, we were frantically trying to make it to Mass on time. As we did before every Mass, we reiterated our rules yet again: "No squirming. No talking. Be respectful, because God's going to be there."

Just as Mass was about to start, we slid into the pew, and as we did, Brady looked at us and asked, "Where's God?"

Before I had time to answer, a man in front of us turned and looked Brady directly in the eye and said gruffly, "He's not here."

Speechless and in shock, I turned to my son to rebut this man's answer, but the music from the entrance song began before I was able to get words out of my mouth. I sat in Mass angered at the man's response. I kept staring at his back, mentally asking, "Why are you here?" Eventually, my anger turned into intense conviction of my belief as I surveyed the church and the people in it—for I saw God everywhere.

I can think of many times when Brady's question was one I was posing: *Where's God?* My guess is that you have experienced such moments or are experiencing one right now, and the question emerges, Where's God in all this? It is to these tough spots of life that we turn now to see how prayer can help hold us steady when life feels turbulent.

Humbled to My Knees

Have you ever had a moment that brought you completely to your knees? October 2012 was like that for me. I was bearing all that was possible for me to bear. In July, we had moved across the country from the small town of Athens, Georgia, to Dallas, Texas, in order for Chris to better his chances of finding a job—and in case you forgot, I really stink at moves. Chris had graduated in May 2012 from his MBA program, and the economy was in a downward spiral. This had an impact not only on my husband's job search but also on our ability to sell our home in Georgia. October marked five months of Chris not having a job and ten months of our home being on the market in Georgia.

The stress of our move and the financial worries came with me as we traveled back to Baton Rouge, Louisiana, one weekend in October to visit family. While there, I visited my friend Peggy, who had pancreatic cancer. She was one of the most influential people in my life, and she is a major reason I entered the ministry. I also visited my grandfather, who had melanoma and lymphoma. When we left my grandfather's house, I turned to Chris with tears in my eyes and said, "We just saw both of them for the last time."

I'll never forget that visit. I barely slept and was extremely restless all weekend. The enormity of all we were facing was too much, and in the middle of my attempting to make sense of it all, God was putting this question on my heart: *What if the answer is no?* I hated this question. I tried my best to dodge it, to push it back to the far crevices of my mind, but God would bring it back to the forefront again. It was as if God were saying, *What if the answer to your request for healing for Peggy and your grandfather is no? What if the answer to your home selling or to Chris's finding a job is no?* I felt like Jacob, wrestling all weekend with this question: *What if the answer is no?*

What was God asking me? God was asking me, *Are you still in if the answer is no? Are you willing to remain in relationship with me if the answers to your prayer requests are no?* For months I had stormed God with prayer requests for clarity of next steps when Chris graduated. I had begged God for a job for Chris. I had pleaded with God to make our house sell in Georgia so we could be unburdened from the financial stress. I had cried out time and time again to God to heal Peggy and my grandfather.

I wrestled with this question—*What if the answer is no?*—on our drive back to Dallas. Sunday night, in the middle of the night, I finally acquiesced. *God, if the answer is no*, I prayed, *I'm still in it. I will still be in a relationship with you.*

In an instant, I felt peace and relief. The wrestling subsided, and I fell into a deep sleep.

I would love to tell you that my anguish was relieved in prayer on that Sunday night and that all the outcomes I prayed for actually occurred, but the reality is, that didn't happen. I received many nos. My grandfather died two days later. Chris went another month without work. Our home was on the market for three more months. Peggy died many months later. Despite bringing all these prayer requests before God, I did not get what I asked for in the way I wanted it all to happen.

What did I gain, though? I gained the assurance of knowing that God was with me in it, and I understood the depth of what it means to say yes to God on a whole new level.

A relationship with God doesn't assure us of a life without suffering. All we have to do is take one look at Jesus on the cross to understand that. But faith and a relationship with God do guarantee us one thing: the abiding presence of God. Pope Francis's words capture it best here:

> Faith is not a light that scatters all our darkness, but a lamp which guides our steps in the night and suffices for the journey. To those who suffer, God does not provide arguments which explain

everything; rather, his response is that of an accompanying presence, a history of goodness which touches every story of suffering and opens up a ray of light.[15]

I experienced God's accompanying presence that weekend as I wrestled with God's question. God reminded me that I was not alone no matter what I faced. God was also teaching me a valuable lesson about faith by asking me if I was still in this relationship if the answer to my prayer was different from what I wanted. This moment took my faith life to a deeper level, to a place of knowing that no matter what, God was with me.

What's more, Jesus understood a thing or two about this.

A Companion for Our Journey

To me, one of the most powerful scenes in the Bible is Jesus in the Garden of Gethsemane. I had heard the words of Jesus in the garden many times, but it wasn't until I was brought to my knees in October 2012 that this scene took on a different meaning for me. Let's look at Luke's description of this scene.

> He came out and went, as was his custom, to the Mount of Olives; and the disciples followed him. When he reached the place, he said to them, "Pray that you may not come into the time of trial." Then he withdrew from them about a stone's throw, knelt down, and prayed, "Father, if you are willing, remove this cup from me; yet, not my will but yours be done." Then an angel from heaven appeared to him and gave him strength. In his anguish he prayed more earnestly, and his sweat became like great drops of blood falling down on the ground. When he got up from prayer, he came to the disciples and found them sleeping because of grief, and he

---

15. Pope Francis, *Lumen Fidei*, paragraph 57, www.vatican.va.

said to them, "Why are you sleeping? Get up and pray that you may not come into the time of trial." (Luke 22:39–46)

What do we see and hear in this scene? This is another example of how the prayer method of Ignatian contemplation can help us get to know Jesus. If we roll through these words without much thought, we miss what is happening. Jesus is praying to his Father to take this cup away from him. This is not a simple, calm prayer. Jesus is praying to the point of his sweat falling like drops of blood.

Jesus, in this moment, though, is teaching us something profound about prayer and a relationship with God. First, Jesus trusts that his Father hears him. Second, Jesus is confident that God has the ability to answer his prayer request. Third, Jesus surrenders to his Father's will. Fourth, Jesus knows he is utterly dependent on God and trusts that God will give him the strength to see his way through what he is facing.

Sometimes what we are facing makes us feel as if we are going through it alone and as if no one else understands our agony or suffering. I have felt like this and still do sometimes: I am going at it alone as I try to walk my way through loss, transition, heartache, grief, or stress.

Jesus gets it. Jesus gets our suffering. He experienced suffering on many levels. He knows what it's like to leave home and go to a foreign land. He knows what it's like to lose friends, both in death (his friend Lazarus) and due to another's actions (Judas, who betrayed him). He knows what it's like when people don't show up the way we want them to; his disciples fell asleep as he prayed in the garden so fervently, and one of his closest friends denied their friendship. Jesus knows what it's like to be questioned when he had done no wrong and to have no one stand up for him. He knows the physical pain that we or our loved ones experience because he experienced it himself during his Passion. He knows what it's like to watch loved ones suffer, because he watched his mother and friends endure the pain of his journey. Jesus knows what it's like to beg like crazy for prayers to be answered and for God to have a different plan.

Because of this, we have a trusted companion for the journey, someone who gets it in a way no one else does. Jesus not only understands what we are going through but also knows what is going on in the depths of our hearts, because he hears our cries and prayers.

Do we trust that God hears our prayers, as Jesus trusted that the Father did? Are we confident that God can answer our prayers? If God does not answer our prayers, do we trust God to give us the strength to get through whatever we're up against? Do we know our dependence on God? These are real questions we face or will face at some point. This is rubber-hits-the-road faith. It's easy to keep the faith when times are good, when life is flowing along at a nice pace. But what about when crisis hits or when we find ourselves in a situation that we have no control over, that nothing we say or do can fix, when no money or other gifts we have can solve the problem? What do we do then? I don't like not having control. I don't like not having the answers. I don't like to feel helpless, where all I can do is cry out to God for help. What do we do when we hit a moment like this?

Jesus, yet again, shows us the way. He turns to God through prayer. Through his example, we learn even more about the value of prayer.

Prayer reminds us we are not alone. God is with us, just as God was with Jesus in the garden.

Prayer offers us a place to voice our needs. God can handle anything: our anger, our pain, our hurt, our suffering, our frustration. God wants our total and utmost honesty, just like the honesty Jesus offered in his garden prayer. This opening of ourselves allows God to enter and meet us.

Prayer builds confidence that God can answer our prayers. Spending time with God strengthens our understanding of God's love for us. As we grow in understanding God's love, our trust in God grows. Over time, we see that God can and does answer our prayers. Jesus spent a tremendous amount of time in prayer with God, and it built his confidence in his Father.

Prayer helps us know our dependence on God. Prayer reminds us that God is the one in control, not us. And as much as we know God is with us, hears us, and answers prayer, we also know that some prayers are not answered the way we want or at all. Jesus experienced this. Jesus got a no when it came to his request that the cup pass from him.

Jesus teaches us about turning to God through prayer in our hard moments and learning to wait in hope. But how do we wait in hope for our prayers to be answered or for the storm to pass? I've learned we can start with the following:

Get silent and pray.

Prayer gives us a landing place and an anchor that reminds us that we are not alone in what we face. It also gives us a place to voice our needs. It allows God to meet us in whatever we are facing and to give us the strength and grace to make it through. Prayer also helps us become more aware of God's voice. We will spend more time on this in the next chapter, but prayer gives us clarity about our next steps. God's voice is in the silence of our hearts.

Name who helps us wait in hope.

Prayers such as the Examen help us become aware of the people who help us on our faith journey. God acts through others. Who helps us wait in hope? Who can help us on our journey? Jesus had people along the way who provided small elements of comfort: Simon, who helped carry his cross; Veronica, who wiped his face; and a slew of disciples, friends, and his mother, who were physically present as he endured his Passion.

Lean on faith tools.

Our faith traditions offer many tools to sustain us as we wait in hope. In my Catholic faith, gifts such as Mass and the sacraments offer nourishment, encouragement, and healing.

Meditate on Scripture.

What Scriptures provide you with strength, faith, and hope? What words do you need to hear as you remember the promises of God?

Build an arsenal of prayer methods.

There is a rich history of prayer traditions in the Catholic faith. What are your go-to prayers that provide comfort and strength for the journey? Might it be the rosary? Or adoration? Are there rote prayers that offer you comfort and hope? Name for yourself what prayer methods you feel drawn to use in difficult times.

While prayer helps us wait in hope, it also provides an anchor for us. Spending time with God reminds us what matters most: the depth of God's love, God's mercy, the fact that we are not abandoned, the reality that our identity is in God and not in any circumstances of our lives, the fact that we are loved as we are and not deemed unworthy by anything we are facing. Prayer anchors us in the truths God has revealed to us.

It also acts as a compass, guiding us one step at a time to our next right step and helping us get through a minute, an hour, or a day at a time if need be. We will talk more at length about this in the next chapter, when we discuss the role that prayer plays in our discernment, but in the realm of walking through tough spots, prayer is our anchor to our dearest friend, Jesus.

Treasured Sorrow

As we close out this chapter on suffering, I want to offer you something that one of my spiritual directors offered me: the gift of a treasured sorrow. A treasured sorrow is a life experience that held both grief and joy. It included pain, challenges, hurt, loss, or grief; yet as we look back on it, we also treasure the experience we went through because of what we learned and who we became in the process. While the experience was a beast to live through, we know the growth we experienced, the reliance on God we now have, and the new awareness we have about ourselves- -awareness we wouldn't have had we not gone through that hard experience.

There are a handful of events in my life I can now name as treasured sorrows. While I would rather not relive those moments of loss and pain, I know that they changed me in a profound way, and so I treasure the lessons I learned.

Because of my treasured sorrows, I am more aware of what others experience. The utter dependency on God during these times grew strong roots of faith that still strengthen me today. I cherish the people I met and the relationships that deepened as we walked the experience together. I know that the tools of my faith offer support and guidance because I leaned on them as I walked the challenging journey.

Our treasured sorrows are our wise teachers, much as Jesus' treasured sorrow taught the world about walking through suffering in hope. With the Holy Spirit's help, we can sift through our experiences and name the sorrows and the treasures. Then, as Ignatian spirituality teaches us, we can offer these experiences to God to be transformed and used by God for the good of others. We will turn now to how prayer helps us in our discernment of what we are called to do, both with treasured sorrows and with any invitation God puts before us.

A Look at Your Life Now

- What are you facing that feels like a tough spot?
- What might your heartfelt prayer look like right now?
- How might Jesus be your companion through whatever you are facing?
- Try to identify some of the treasured sorrows in your life.

Pray with Jesus in the garden (Luke 22:39–46) using Lectio Divina or Ignatian contemplation.

Prepare to wait in hope. Who will help you wait in hope? What Scriptures can you turn to that will support you on this journey? What prayer tools will you use? What other tools of your faith might help right now (sacraments, Mass, etc.)?

9

Sent Forth

Write! Go write for Me! Share with others what I've taught you.

These words resounded in me as I entered the fourth week of the Spiritual Exercises. It was not a new call for me, though, as it was one that arose during the first week of the Spiritual Exercises as I prayed with the questions of the first week: *What have I done for Christ? What am I doing for Christ? What ought I do for Christ?* The pull and the tug to write was growing immensely as I now prayed with the Resurrection Gospel stories in the fourth week. As Jesus appeared to his disciples after his resurrection, he sent his disciples forth to continue his mission. And as much as I did not want to believe it or accept it, Jesus was sending me forth to spread his mission, too, through writing.

I should tell you this: I hated English class. I hated writing papers in high school and college. My sophomore English teacher was tough, and often my papers were returned with Cs, despite the effort I put into them. Both my high school and my college major required oodles of papers and essays, and my master's program through Loyola University in New Orleans required multiple essays per class as a way of synthesizing and applying what I learned.

I share this because as this call to write became more pronounced, I was not excited to hear it. I heard the voices of my past telling me that my writing was not the greatest, and I also knew the immense amount of work it always takes for me to process information internally in a way that allows me to get it out on paper. So as I encountered Jesus in his Resurrection stories, I was surprised as all get-out to discover that writing emerged as the call and that this was one of the ways Jesus was sending me forth to spread what I had received through our relationship.

Prayer Calls Us Outward

I don't know what I was thinking at this point on my faith journey. Perhaps I was hoping prayer was meant just for me and God. I knew it made me feel warm, cozy, loved, and healed. I knew it helped me see God in all things and receive God's mercy and lean on God when the going got tough. It surprised me, though, to experience prayer calling me *outward* and to learn that prayer was about action—not just God's action, but yours and mine.

As I mentioned in a previous chapter, Ignatian spirituality names this outward call as being a *contemplative in action*. As men and women in the world, we can be people of prayer (that's the contemplative part), but we are also called to be people of action. Prayer is going to call us outward. God is going to give us a task—a unique role—in the mission of spreading the Good News of Jesus. These roles and callings are not just for priests or religious men and women. They are for every one of us.

God uses our gifts, our life experiences, and all our understanding for the good of the world. What I experienced as I ended the Spiritual Exercises was deep gratitude for all God has done and does in my life. At the same time, I experienced a tug and a nudge to be sent forth and to take what had happened in prayer outward, to share with others.

A Courageous Prayer

A prayer that accompanies a person making the Spiritual Exercises in the fourth week is called the "Take, Lord" prayer. Before I share the words of this prayer, I want to give you another warning: If you want to keep your life exactly the way it is, then I suggest you not pray this prayer. Prayer transforms us because of our encounter with Christ, and through this encounter with Christ, we are sent to encounter others. This prayer will have an impact on your life because of the way it deepens your reliance on God and not on the gifts God gives us and because of the way it offers all that we have received for God's use.

Here are the beautiful words of the prayer penned by St. Ignatius:

> Take, Lord, and receive all my liberty,
> my memory, my understanding,
> and my entire will.
> All I have and call my own.
>
> You have given all to me.
> To you, Lord, I return it.
>
> Everything is yours; do with it what you will.
> Give me only your love and your grace,
> that is enough for me.
> Amen.

This was the prayer I prayed as the nudge to write grew stronger. This was the prayer I prayed as I understood my foundation to be built solely on God and not on any of the gifts God gave me. I prayed for God to use all that I have and call my own. I prayed that Jesus would take all my memories, my understanding, my life experiences, and my will and use them. I prayed that I could cling to God for my value and not measure my worth by the experiences, memories, or gifts given to me. I prayed this prayer out of gratitude for all God had done in my life up to that point and all God had given me. I prayed this prayer out of gratitude for walking so closely with Jesus through his Passion and for understanding in a new way what the Crucifixion meant and how this was done out of God's deep love for us. The "Take, Lord" prayer moved me to awe as I surveyed my life and looked at all the ways God had moved and worked in me and labored on my behalf.

I yearned to reflect into the world all that God did for me out of his tenacious love. I wanted to reflect that love to others.

God answered my prayer and sent me forth. This book is one of the many fruits of God answering my prayer—the fruit not only of my prayer life but also of the many life experiences God helped me through and the multitude of people God put into my life to help me grow spiritually. They are all gifts from God, and I yearned to do something to thank God for them.

At the end of the *Exercises*, St. Ignatius says this about love: "First, love shows itself in deeds more than words. Second, love is a mutual sharing so that the lover always gives to and receives from the beloved everything—gifts, money, convictions, honors and position."[16] What I experienced as I ended the Spiritual Exercises is what I notice weekly as I listen to people talk about their relationship with God and their prayer lives: the call outward. A desire grows to do something for God out of the love received, mercy bestowed, and gifts given. Even if you never make the Spiritual Exercises, I assure you that if you are a woman or man of prayer, God is going to send you forth and give you a concrete call to be part of his work on earth.

Our Unique, Concrete Contribution

What happened to me through my relationship with God is my own story and the particular way God invites me to contribute to God's work in the world. You have your own story too, and your own set of

---

16. Joseph A. Tetlow, SJ, *Choosing Christ in the World* (Boston: Institute for Jesuit Sources, 1999), 172–73.

gifts, desires, and experiences. God will raise that desire and give you the gifts and means to act on it.

Here are a few basic principles I want you to remember as you look at what your concrete contribution might be:

Unique call

In a unique, concrete way, each of us contributes to building God's kingdom. A person lives out this contribution through a vocational role as a single or married person, as a religious sister or brother, or as a priest. This means we have a contribution to make with regard to raising children, the professional work we do, and the organizations we are involved in. This also applies to our small, day-to-day dealings: how we interact with other people, how we handle our money, and what we do with our time.

Desires of the heart

God helps us know our concrete contributions through the desires of the heart, and God awakens and stimulates these desires. I like to think of it as God raising in us the desire to do the next good thing.

Our gifts

God gives us the gifts we need to act on our desires. God will not only give us the gifts but will also give us the means and opportunities to act on them. This goes back to how we are uniquely made and loved. Each of us has a particular set of gifts, skills, knowledge, and experiences that ready us to do God's kingdom-work in this world. One honest point I want to make is that sometimes God gives us the desires of our hearts, but there is a long waiting period before they come to fruition. This is when we can use some of the suggestions offered in chapter 8 about how to wait in hope and stay grounded in prayer.

Our free will

Each of us has free will. We can choose to act on our desires or not. That's the option God gives us. Just remember, knowing our desires and not acting on them is most likely going to create a world of desolation, unrest, disquiet, and anything *but* inner peace!

As you look at these principles, I invite you to reflect on each of them and name for yourself what you notice in your own life. What are your responsibilities? What are your natural gifts, the activities that bring you joy? Is there a desire that God is inviting you to pay attention to? Is God opening up the means and ways for you to use your gifts to act on this desire?

At times, trying to act on our true desires can feel overwhelming. Sometimes discernment can feel so big that I don't know where to start or which steps to take. Let's turn now to breaking discernment down into smaller pieces and how prayer can support us in this process.

What Is the Next Right Step?

When I was growing up, my dad would often remind me when I was feeling overwhelmed, "Becky, how do you eat an elephant?" The correct answer: "One bite at a time." I am notorious for trying to solve everything at once, especially when it comes to discernment. I want the whole picture figured out, the vision made clear, and my beginning and ending fully known.

Discernment, though, happens in bites. Often all we can ask God is, *What is my next right step?*

Discernment is like making a good meal of red beans and rice. When I first start to cook the red beans and rice, my big stock pot is up front and center on the largest burner. I turn the heat on high, add a little oil, and throw in bunches of onion, bell pepper, and celery. The vegetables need tending as they soften—I stir pretty regularly so they don't stick to the bottom of the pot. Once the veggies are ready, the rest of the ingredients get dumped in: beans, sausage, chicken broth, and lots of seasoning.

With all the ingredients in place, I put the lid on the pot, push the pot to the back of the stove, and lower the heat. The beans simmer for hours before they are ready to eat.

Throughout the cooking process, I lift the lid from time to time to check on the water level and to stir the beans. While they are simmering, I cook the rice and cornbread. Perhaps I cook a side dish as well. Each requires a different pot and place on the stove, and each requires a certain amount of heat. I see every pot on the stove. I tend to the one that needs my attention the most, and then I push it to the back or lower the heat. I continue to do this until the meal is ready to serve.

The same is true for our discernment. On our discernment stove, there might be several dishes to which God invites our discernment and attention. God sees every pot that is cooking. When God wants our attention about one certain pot, God turns up the heat to get our attention. Maybe it boils over before we notice that we're being invited to tend to it. God moves the pot that needs our attention at the time to the front and center of our stove. We might be invited to notice it, check the heat, throw in a few more ingredients, stir it a bit, and push it back to simmer some more. At some point, though, we will be invited to take it off the stove—either to get rid of it completely or to savor and enjoy what's been created.

God's there through it all, watching over all aspects of my life, like one of my kids watching me cook, sneaking a taste, calling out if it boils over or scorches on the bottom or needs a little more heat.

I think we sometimes worry that if we are not tending to a pot, it's going to go away. That's not the case, though. If God wants that pot on the stove, it's not going anywhere. That's why I always boil discernment down to this: What is the next right step? Our next right step might be shoving the pot to the back and letting it simmer some more. Perhaps our next right step is gathering a bit more information and throwing it into the pot. Or maybe we are called to turn up the heat on our discernment by actively making a choice.

Prayer and Discernment

What is the role of prayer in our discernment? First and foremost, prayer grounds us. Prayer gives us our solid footing. Prayer is how we come to know God's presence in us and in our world, and it's how we come to know God's love for us and God's gift of mercy for us. Prayer is how we come to know God's voice through being with God and sitting with God's Word, the Scriptures, all of which fine-tune our ear for God. Prayer is how we come to know Jesus and how Jesus models for us how to live in the reality of our situations and to walk through suffering.

Prayer, though, is also how we are sent to go outside ourselves. Prayer makes our actions holy and gives us eyes to see all people as holy. It spurs us beyond ourselves to take part in God's mission. Jesus' disciples discovered a taste of this as they were sent forth by Jesus in the conclusion of the Gospel of Matthew:

> "Go therefore and make disciples of all nations, baptizing them in the name of the Father and of the Son and of the Holy Spirit, and teaching them to obey everything that I have commanded you. And remember, I am with you always, to the end of the age." (Matt. 28:19–20)

The disciples spent almost three years with Jesus, working with him closely and getting to know him as an intimate friend. When Jesus died, they grieved the loss of their close friend. When Jesus rose from the dead and appeared to the disciples, he comforted them and then sent them forth to preach and make new disciples.

Jesus sends us forth also. Each of us is sent forth to use our gifts to further Jesus' mission today. The blessing of our prayer lives is that we are not sent forth on our own; rather, we are sent forth with a trusted companion at our side: Jesus. In addition, we have the gift of the Holy Spirit that Jesus asked his Father to send us. The Holy Spirit gently nudges us on to answer our call of where we are sent.

Your "Greater Yes"

In his *Spiritual Exercises*, St. Ignatius offers us two sets of rules for discernment. His first set is focused entirely on whether or not our lives are oriented toward God and around God. This set of rules focuses on a choice between good and evil. The gift of this set of rules helps us know what leads us toward God and what draws us away from God.

His second set of rules presumes that a person is living a life of prayer and is engaged in a dynamic relationship with God. This set of rules is about helping the other person choose between two goods. The key discernment question here is, *Which is the greater good?*

If you are reading this book, then probably you have already made the basic choice between good and evil; you have chosen to orient your life toward God. So I am going to focus primarily on the second set of rules. And to do so, I'm going to tell you more about my friend Peggy.

Peggy and I worked together at the Diocese of Baton Rouge. However, I first met Peggy when I was seventeen years old, and she walked with me through many major decisions: what major to choose in college, how to handle difficult family situations, and how to discern my vocational and ministry calls. I would seek her advice on matters great and small. Whatever the decision, Peggy would boil down my discernment to one question: "What is your greater yes?"

Peggy did not have the education of a Jesuit or the experience of someone like St. Ignatius, but the question she offered me and so many others for discernment captures the essence of Ignatian discernment: Which choice will lead me closer to God? Or which is the better way? Knowing this is not always easy, but fortunately St. Ignatius offers us some keys to discerning what God asks of us—namely through the discernment of spirits.

Ignatius's basis for discernment is the belief that God is at work in our lives and speaks to us through the Holy Spirit. God uses our emotions, our feelings, and our intellect to help us know the next right step for us. Ignatius also teaches, as do most Christian traditions, that there is an evil spirit at work in our lives as well—the spirit not of God, which some call Satan or the devil. Ignatius spent his life refining how to discern between the two spirits.

If we are living a life of faith and are open to God, which we have spent a good portion of this book discussing, then the Holy Spirit confirms our choices by giving us peace about our decisions. In this case, the evil spirit tries to get us off our path of growing closer to God by creating doubts. If we are *not* living a life of faith, the Holy Spirit disturbs us and shakes us up with feelings of remorse to help us get back on track and make choices that help us grow closer to God. In this case, the evil spirit tries to console us to continue on our path that takes us away from God.

Sound confusing? Trust me, I know it can be! But to help us, Ignatius offers insight into two key experiences: consolation and desolation.

We experience consolation any time we feel an increase of faith, hope, and love. I often ask my directees to notice if any of the fruits of the Spirit are present. Do you notice love, joy, peace, patience, kindness, goodness, faithfulness, gentleness, and self-control as you pray about a choice? If you're considering an option that will help you grow closer to God, then the Holy Spirit encourages you "by making all easy, by removing all obstacles so that the soul goes forward in doing good" (*Spiritual Exercises*, #315).

We experience desolation when we feel a decrease of faith, hope, and love. If we do not feel the fruits of the Spirit, it's a sign that we are not on the right path. If things feel hard, as though doors are closing, or if we want to keep things secret, we may be in desolation and not considering the right course. We may also have a loss of energy and be full of doubt.

Through prayer, we can pay attention and notice if we are experiencing consolation or desolation. When we consider a choice God is putting before us, we can notice if we are feeling an increase of faith, hope, and love or a decrease of these things. You will find that even choices that seem hard will carry with them the gift of inner peace if the decision is the right one.

A spiritual director can be a wonderful companion in helping you discern. Most spiritual directors, like myself, go through intensive programs to learn about how to help another person discern.

Four Steps of Discernment

Beyond noticing consolation and desolation, we can also take some formal steps to walk through a process of discernment. To describe these steps, I will use the model offered by Mark Thibodeaux, SJ, in his book *God's Voice Within*, which I find to be one of the best discernment books available. I have used his steps through the years, adapting the wording somewhat. These are the four steps I walk people through in spiritual direction if a directee is seeking to make a choice between two goods.

1. Pray

By this point, I hope you know how to get quiet and find some soli-tude to be with God. Within the silence, talk to God about the choice you're seeking to make. Talk to God about what you desire, what your hopes are, and what your fears are. Then let God speak to you.

Notice what arises in prayer. Pray to do God's will and for God to increase your trust in God's help to guide your decision and for God to give you the courage to act when it's clear to do so. No choice we make in prayer is made alone. God is with us in our decisions. It may be helpful as you pray to seek out another person, such as a spiritual director, to pray and discern with you.

2. Gather Data

The second step of discernment is to gather data. The data includes both the hard-core facts that affect your decision as well as your emo-tions and feelings. St. Ignatius offers many suggestions when we are at this phase of discernment:

Start with what you know. What invitation is God putting forth for you to discern? Name the facts, such as the specific choice in front of you. What are the "costs," if there are any, to making this choice (this includes financial cost as well as things such as reloca-tion or changes in relationships)? At this stage, you list the hard facts about the choice. Then consider, Who else will be affected by this decision? Do you need to invite anyone else into this discernment process with you? For example, because I'm married, I do not dis-cern alone; I discern with God and with Chris, and every choice we make has an impact on our three children.

Pay attention to the movement of the spirits. This means noticing where you feel consolation and desolation. When, in your prayer and pondering, do you feel consolation—an increase of faith, hope, and love? When do you feel desolation—a decrease of faith, hope, and love?

Make a pro-and-con list. Weigh the pros and cons of the choices. Include in this list the costs of each option as well as the possible benefits of each option.

Act as if you made the decision. Ponder what life would be like if you acted on one of the choices. Then ponder what life would be like if you made the other choice. Notice which way brings more of an increase of faith, hope, and love.

Act as if you were giving advice to someone else. St. Ignatius offers this practical way of looking at choices: Pretend a friend came to you with your same discernment dilemma. What advice would you give that friend? What would it feel like if you took that advice to heart and acted on it for your life?

Imagine yourself at your death. St. Ignatius also suggests that you imagine that you're at the end of your life. As you look back on this decision, which choice will matter more in the end?

You may employ all these methods in your discernment process or just one or two of them. The main thing, as you go about gathering data, is that you take the information back to prayer, talking to God about what you are noticing and the information you are gathering. Continue to ask God for clarity of choice.

3. Come to a Decision

At some point, God will make the choice clear to you. It may be through overwhelming consolation—that deep inner peace—or it may be just a gut knowing. It may be that the facts of the decision cleared the way for you to make a choice. When you are ready, prayerfully commit to your decision and let God affirm your decision in prayer. Continue to ask God, *Is this my next right step? Is this what you desire?*

I also suggest sharing your decisions with a few trusted external voices. Are they in agreement with your decision? Are they affirming your discernment? As you commit to your decision, notice the fruits of your decision. Is there consolation as you consider making this choice? Are you at peace? Are things opening up and aligning themselves for you to take this course of action? Ignatius suggests that if things keep closing, as opposed to easily opening, we need to pay attention to whether this is the right choice or not.

4. Act

Once your decision is affirmed in prayer, then act on it. Continue to ask God to give you clarity and confirmation as you live into your decision. Check the fruits of your decision as you live into it. Are you still feeling consolation? Are you noticing increases of faith, hope, and love within you and within those who were affected by your choice? Continue to do this until you feel clarity in making this choice.

The Examen's Role

I first introduced the Examen in chapter 4, where we talked about how it can help us see God in all things. Next, we talked in chapter 6 about how the Examen can help us become aware of when we are in need of God's mercy, of our sins, and of when we are struggling to name God's presence in our lives. Now I want us to look at how the Examen can help us in our discernment.

The Examen's role in discernment is threefold. First, this prayer method can help us name our gifts. Second, it can help us name the desires of heart. Third, it can give clarity about our next right steps.

Let's review the steps of the Examen quickly: (For full Examen description see pages 45–47.)

1. Ask for the Holy Spirit's help.

2. Be thankful.

3. Notice God's presence.

4. Notice the lack of God's presence.

5. Look to the future.

Each day, the Examen invites us to see our day and ourselves as God sees it. The Examen can help us notice our gifts and our desires. As we review our day in prayer, we might thank God for a time we got to do something we enjoy, are good at, and are passionate about. We might notice whom we enjoy spending our time with and whom we do not. We may notice activities and tasks that bring us life and those we cannot stand to do or those that drain our energy and decrease our faith.

If we pray the Examen daily, we will begin to notice patterns and things that recur, and these will give us direction on what our next right step might be, which will ultimately lead to us living out the deepest desires of our heart and acting on the concrete contribution God hopes we will give to the kingdom.

✝

Living lives of prayer helps us not only build a relationship with God but also discern our response to God's love for us and our love for God. No matter how or where we are called to use our unique gifts, being in relationship with God and doing what God asks brings us the gift of joy. And that's where we turn now, to the grace of joy that comes from being in an intimate relationship with God.

A Look at Your Life Now

- How do I feel myself being called outward and sent forth by God? (What is the call? What are my gifts? What are the desires of my heart?)
- What is the right next step in my discernment?
- What is my greater yes?

Use the four steps of discernment on pages 114–116, and apply them to a decision you are trying to make.

10

Embracing the Railways

Our society talks a lot about happiness. Social media touts such ideas as "Three steps to happiness" or "Keys to living a happy life." I'm turned off because these promises seem cheap and shallow. They do not take into account the multitude of life's twists and turns. Sadly, I hear and read many Christian preachers and teachers declaring the "prosperity Gospel," which claims that if you believe in God and live just the right way, you will be prosperous and happy. These messages get under my skin because they make it seem as if living a life of faith means completing a series of steps to achieve happiness and that doing so somehow protects you from suffering. This misses the depth of our human longing, which is to be loved freely and unconditionally and not to be alone.

I want us to consider a different way of looking at happiness. In this chapter we are going to talk about *joy*, not happiness. In my opinion, happiness is the empty promise that our society offers us: you'll be happy when you find the right person to marry or buy the right car or earn a certain amount of money. Joy, however, is the promise of God, a fruit of the Holy Spirit. Joy is a gift from God, a grace given to us through prayer. Like any gift from God, it is not earned but freely given.

Joy is a powerful gift that we carry in our interior chapel, and it grows out of a life lived with God and not apart from God. Joy comes from being rooted in a relationship with God that keeps us grounded when the going gets tough or when everything feels dark. Joy is a source of light and hope that can radiate into every aspect of life. Joy does not eliminate our troubles and pain, but it allows us to carry a deep hope and a confidence that no matter what, God will get us through our troubles and pain. Pope Francis says, "Joy is a sign that the Gospel is bearing fruit."[17]

You probably know at least one or two people who are full of joy. I can name several; I call these men and women Resurrection People.

Resurrection People

Resurrection People exude joy no matter the circumstances. These people live a faith that attracts others. They seem to possess a depth and a groundedness. Their eyes dance with joy that seems untouchable. If you listen to their stories, you hear about plenty of hurt and hardship. But you also hear a quiet, strong confidence in someone other than themselves as they share about how God carried them through many tough times. Their eyes are framed by the lines of life but keep their sparkle of joy. It is obvious they have encountered the risen Jesus.

My faith journey was spurred along by the influence of many Resurrection People. Gazing into the eyes of these friends, mentors, and colleagues, I encountered my own longing for what they seemed to possess: an unshakable confidence in God, a faith that attracts others like a magnet, and a positivity that radiates out of their every move and expression.

---

17. Pope Francis, *The Joy of the Gospel* (Frederick, Md.: The Word Among Us, 2013), 24. Also available at www.vatican.va, paragraph 21.

My friend Peggy, whom I mentioned in the previous two chapters, was a Resurrection Person. Her influence on my life was profound as she taught me how to walk through suffering and live my greater yes. There is one more lesson, though, that she taught me, and I believe that every person needs to hear it.

Two Railways

Peggy and I went to lunch one day when we both worked at the Diocese of Baton Rouge, she a woman in her fifties and I in my twenties. As we often did, we moved quickly from superficial chitchat to digging deep. We listened and shared with each other about what was happening in our work and our families. At the time, there was a very difficult situation in my extended family, and yet Chris and I were newlyweds and leaning into our new life as a couple. I shared how I felt that I was living a paradox. I was dealing with one of the hardest situations I had ever experienced and at the same time going through that most joyous experience of beginning life as a married couple with Chris.

That day, Peggy shared with me an image that has helped me again and again.

"Becky, I often think of life like a train track," she said. "There are two rails on that track. One rail represents all the good things in life and the places we easily experience God. The other rail represents the places in which it seems hard to find God or see the good."

She went on to say the two rails run alongside each other simultaneously to make up the track. At times, one rail may feel more obvious in our life. Perhaps we are overwhelmed with love, kindness, beauty, peace, and hope—and it's hard to notice that the other rail exists. Other times we may find ourselves so overwhelmed with pain and suffering that we cannot see that the first rail exists.

But in reality, both rails exist all the time.

What connects the two rails? Train tracks are connected by cross-beams. Peggy suggested that the two ongoing realities in life are connected by prayer. God is present in both rails and connects the two for us. It is through prayer that we can find and name God through the good moments and in our suffering. It is through prayer that we do not become so blinded by God's gift of joy that we forget about the suffering of others or act as if our own suffering does not exist. The two rails come together as we offer all aspects of life to God through prayer and as God begins to show us how both rails are necessary to move us forward and continue on a deepened journey of faith.

As Peggy finished describing the train-rail image, she said, "I know that in real life, train rails do not move closer together, but in our faith lives I believe that the further we grow in our relationship with God, the closer the two rails are to each other. It becomes easier to name God in all of it. That's what brings me joy."

Not All "Peachy Roses"

Peggy shared that image with me almost thirteen years ago, and I still hold it closely. It is an image I share often with people in spiritual direction. And I think it is a fitting image for the last chapter of this book.

Part of seeing God in all things is noticing God at work everywhere, in both the good and the not-so-good. Peggy carried joy and nurtured the gift of joy in her life even though she had her fair share of ups and downs. Her joy didn't come from a life free of pain but rather from a life rooted in Jesus. She knew that no matter what she faced, Jesus would be with her in it and get her through it.

This was the attitude she carried as she lived two years with pancreatic cancer—a journey full of "happy-sad moments," where the two rails were very apparent. The last time I talked to her was just weeks before she passed away. I asked her, "Peggy, what can I pray for you?" Her reply was, "Pray that I continue to live gratefully and with continuous joy." She understood what it meant to live as a woman of faith. Her motto was to live and love abundantly based on her favorite verse, John 10:10: "I came that they may have life and have it abundantly."

Peggy proclaimed the gospel as she lived an abundant life anchored in God. She knew that the gift of joy does not mean that all is "peachy roses" but that we can feel at peace and close to God no matter what we are facing and that we can name God at work no matter what is going on in our lives. Peggy was not a saint or a priest or a religious sister or brother. She was like most of us reading this book: a layperson, a woman of prayer who encountered Christ and whose life was transformed because of that encounter.

The joy that Peggy carried within is offered to each of us. It is the fruit of the Spirit, and people who carry it draw people to them with a magnetic pull that we cannot logically understand. When we encounter someone who is full of joy, we encounter God. I don't know about you, but I want to live as Peggy did, with my life bearing fruit through my joy. I want people to encounter God when they meet me. What Peggy taught me requires no degree or credentials. Her formula was simple: prayer and encountering the risen Christ.

The Joy of the Risen Christ

As we talked about in an earlier chapter, Jesus was human like us, which means he experienced the range of emotions and life circumstances that we do in life. Jesus had a family and lived in a community. He had friends and people he loved and cared for in his life. Jesus, as a human, experienced the pain and hurt of his Passion and death. He was laid to rest, just as we will be one day.

But Jesus' story does not end with being laid to rest in the tomb. Holy Saturday is not the end but just a period of waiting. Today, because we know the whole story, it's hard to imagine the agony that Jesus' disciples and family felt as he breathed his last breath on the cross and was laid to rest in the tomb. Maybe we get glimpses of this when we are caught up in a moment in life where it feels as if Easter is never coming. Today, we know that Easter Sunday comes and that Jesus is resurrected from the dead.

Jesus' resurrection is so ingrained in the makeup of our Christian story that at times I feel we take it for granted and lack a deep understanding of what it really means. We are often like the disciples when Jesus appeared to them, our eyes closed or blinded to seeing the new life in front of us in the person of the risen Christ.

The Resurrection changed everything. It is through the Resurrection that we understand Jesus' divinity and that Jesus is not only human but also divine. The risen Christ is a man who experienced the Passion as a human man yet overcame death and rose. The risen Christ embodies God's desire to go to any extremes on our behalf out of God's love for us. Evil did not prevail. God did. God counteracted the human acts of the people of Jesus' time in the most unexpected way: the Resurrection. The risen Christ is the Jesus we know today, the one who fully embraces both his humanity and divinity.

What does the Resurrection mean for us? It means that we will never be alone. Jesus is still with us through his gift of the Holy Spirit, the great Advocate. It means that God is not going to leave us to our own devices, chance, or fate, but that God is with us and actively working in our world today. It means that God can overcome anything, even his Son's death on the cross, and birth new life. I don't know about you, but that is something I need to hear over and over again. I want it to sink into my bones that God can birth new life out of any situation and that I am never alone because of the gift of friendship with Jesus.

It is my own personal encounter with the risen Christ that helps me walk through life with hope. It is my relationship with God, nurtured through my prayer life, that helps me see everything as holy. Prayer helped me know God intimately and understand that God is in all things. When I look around me, I see God everywhere—in me, in others, and in the world.

When I consider all I have lived through so far, the grace of joy deepens in me because of all God has brought me through. When I think of all the ways God has kept me from falling on my face or forgave me for a wrong or tended to a wound or hurt, joy deepens in me. I often look at my life and wonder, *How am I still standing? How was this event or that thing I did or said not the end of me?* It is simply because of God. Every time I thought I was at my end, God came in and lifted me up. Every time I was at the end of my rope, God offered me more. Every time there seemed to be no way out, God offered an alternative door.

I'm changed because of my encounters with God, Jesus, and the Holy Spirit that have come through my prayer life. I forgave and forgive people I never thought I could, because of God's help. I loved people and love people that at times seem unlovable to me, because God helps me. I, for sure, have done things I never dreamed of doing, because of God. People question me all the time because of my age at pursuing a life of prayer during the season of life I am in. They imply that my relationship with God should somehow be delayed to a later season, when my kids are no longer in my house or when my professional career is further along. I cannot count the number of times people have, to my face, questioned the ministry work I do, causing immense doubt in me. Every time, though, I bring this doubt to God in prayer, and God affirms my call to both be in relationship with God and to do the work I do.

So this is why I am here, now, writing this book. Because I hope that you hear a different message from me than I heard at times. The time for prayer is now. I do not care what is going on in your life—if you are raising kids or are an empty nester. I don't care if you are working eighteen hours a day seven days a week or are faced with hours of loneliness a day. It doesn't matter if you are young or old, single or married, religious or ordained. The time for prayer is now. God will meet you where you are and work within the reality of your life to bring you closer to God. God meets you, all of you, in all of your life.

How can I not have joy when I look at my life and all the ways God has showed up and continues to show up, has worked and is working in me, has called and calls me, has healed and heals me, has loved and continues—every moment—to love me? The source of my joy is my relationship with God that is nurtured by a prayer life. This gift of joy carries me. It calls me to new places. It sustains me when no one and nothing else can. It supports me when I'm full of doubt.

The gift of joy keeps growing the longer I carefully tend my relationship with God. Every time I witness God at work within me or another person, joy grows. Every time I witness an unbelievable act of goodness, it grows. My prayer for each of us is that our faith lives can attract others the way so many others' lives did for me, and that we, too, can help others understand that everything is holy.

A Look at Your Life Now

- Who are the Resurrection People in my life?
- Where am I embracing the "two rails"?
- How did I encounter the risen Christ? Where do I experience joy?

Go live as a Resurrection Person! What would need to change for this to happen?

Acknowledgments

I'm so grateful that we do not walk our faith journeys alone. This book came to fruition due to the impact of many people who walked with me over the years, shared their love of God with me, and gave me the prayer tools to make my relationship with God an integral part of my life.

To my mom and dad, Cookie and Kerry Uffman, for giving me a solid faith foundation both at home and through the gift of Catholic education. To my brothers and sisters-in-law, for keeping me humble, laughing, and grounded in reality, and for asking me challenging questions about faith. To my grandparents, John and Carolyn Perkins, for modeling what it means to be generous and for reinforcing my faith foundation. To the Uffman family, for teaching me to see God in all things, especially in nature. To Debbie and George Eldredge, for your support through your gift of time with our children, which gave me space to grow in my knowledge of faith, to lead retreats, to attend retreats, and to write.

To the Sisters of St. Joseph, for overseeing my faith formation in elementary and high school and for introducing me to Ignatian spirituality. To my religion teachers, Crystal Eldringhoff, Mary Jo Raborn, and Judy Lavergne for inspiring me to get to *know* Jesus through your teaching, your questions, and your models of faith. To Sr. Ily

Fernandez, CSJ, my first spiritual director, for teaching me how to pray with Scripture and for remaining a dear friend and ministry colleague.

To Fr. John Carville, for inviting me to attend Catholic Leadership Institute and bringing the great trio of Charles Jumonville, Cooper Ray, and Peggy Leblanc into my life. The three of them changed the trajectory of my life both through their ministry at the Diocese of Baton Rouge Youth Office as well as through the community of people they welcomed me into. To Charles, for inviting me into professional ministry. To Coop, for mentoring me and taking me under your wing in regard to retreat ministry. To Peggy, for profoundly impacting my life through your joy, love, and ability to see God in all people and situations; I carry something of you each person I encounter.

To all who have walked with me as spiritual directors, honoring my desire to grow in God and arming me with tools from Ignatian spirituality to walk through marriage, motherhood, ministry, and many transitions in this past decade of life: Sr. Ily Fernandez, CSJ, Sr. Jackie Bates, r.c., Bob Fitzgerald, and Diane Millis. To Jim Maloney for guiding me through the Spiritual Exercises and for never blinking at the fact that I started them with a four week old in my arms.

To my Charis family: Jenéne Francis, Lauren Gaffey, Pam Coster, Fr. Michael Sparough, SJ, Lauren Berke, Megan Kennedy-Farrell, Mary Ellen Madden, Lisa Sroka, Jesse Keane, Anne Williams, and all the Charis Partners. Your gift of friendship, your shared heart for retreats and the Spiritual Exercises, and your desire to bring Ignatian spirituality to new audiences changed forever the way I do ministry. Thank you for deepening my call to work with the Spiritual Exercises and Ignatian spirituality.

To all who were part of my journey through the Loyola University of New Orleans Institute for Ministry Program and the Spring Hill

College Spiritual Direction program: you gave me language to understand what was always within me, and you armed me with discernment wisdom and faith tools that help me personally and professionally.

To the parish communities that welcomed our family, gave us a place to call home, and strengthened our faith foundation, St. Jean Vianney in Baton Rouge, The Catholic Center at the University of Georgia, St. Rita in Dallas, and St. Aloysius in Baton Rouge. To Fr. Tom Vigliotta, OFM, for believing in me and encouraging me to become a spiritual director, even if I thought you were crazy—and told you so on numerous occasions—to send people twice my age to meet with me. To Fr. Tom Ranzino and Msgr. Bob Coerver for your support and encouragement to continue in the ministry of spiritual direction and retreats.

To the Loyola Press team: Ray Ives, Denise Gorss, Rosemary Lane, Tom McGrath, Steve Connor, Becca Russo, Yvonne Micheletti, and Andrew Yankech; you continue to encourage and stretch me in new ways to say yes to God's dreams within me. To Vinita Wright: your adept editing eye made me a better writer and helped me blend my writing and my retreat ministry with your suggestion to add "A Look at Your Life Now" at the end of each chapter. To Joe Durepos, who I wanted to scream at on more than one occasion during this five-year writing journey but who would not accept anything less than my best; I am deeply thankful for your mentorship and for helping me believe in myself.

To Mark Thibodeaux, SJ, for not only writing the foreword to this book but also for your encouraging words throughout this writing process. No matter what you say, I am still convinced that your South Louisiana accent is thicker than mine.

To Marcie Buckle, Missy Devillier, Stephanie Clouatre-Davis, Fr. Michael Alello, Wendi Fanucci, Mary Mahaffey, David Briones, and Mandy Makin; your friendships help hold me steady and grounded in what matters most. To Musick, for encouraging me to start writing and believing in me before I believed in myself; I remain thankful to call you friend and family.

To Christianne Squires: there are no words to say thank you for our kindred-hearted friendship. You were a midwife to this book for over two years through your friendship, your discernment wisdom, and your editing skills. This book is what it is today because of your gift to call out what was deep within me. To Christine Mason Miller: you popped into my life as an unexpected gift and helped me birth this book within the reality of life by teaching me the tools and providing your example of writing in the busyness of life.

To all whom I met on retreats, at talks or workshops, and to all who share their stories with me during spiritual direction: your faces, hearts, stories, and questions were with me as I wrote this book. Thank you for being in my life.

To St. Ignatius, for the gifts of your spirituality and for your discernment wisdom that touch every aspect of my life.

To Brady, Abby, and Mary; you are God's concrete example of love and light in this world. Being your mom is a gift, and I am thankful for all the ways you influence how I live my life and how I learn to love and be loved.

To Chris, to whom this book is dedicated. This book would not have come out of my mind and heart if it were not for your relentless belief in it and in me. You never gave up on me or on my ability to get the words out, even when I did. Thank you for "getting" me, loving me, supporting me, challenging me, and helping me cultivate space for prayer in the middle of our beautiful and full life. I love you!

About the Author

Becky is a spiritual director, retreat facilitator, and writer. She helps others create space to connect faith and everyday life through facilitating retreats and days of reflection, through writing and spiritual direction.

Drawing on more than fifteen years of ministry experience in the Catholic Church, Becky seeks to help others discover God at work in the everyday moments of their lives by utilizing St. Ignatius's Spiritual Exercises and the many gifts that Ignatian Spirituality provides.

Becky currently lives in Baton Rouge, Louisiana, where she meets with men and women of all ages for monthly spiritual direction and leads people through the Spiritual Exercises of St. Ignatius. She leads retreats and days of reflection for parishes and other ministry organizations, and she gives Ignatian preached retreats at various retreat houses.

In addition, she offers reflections series and weekly reflections on her website, www.beckyeldredge.com, as well as bi-weekly reflections on Loyola Press' Ignatian Spirituality blog, dotMagis.

She shares life with her husband, Chris, and their three children: Brady, Abby, and Mary.

Ignatian Spirituality Online
www.ignatianspirituality.com

Visit us online to

- Join our *E-Magis* newsletter

- Pray the Daily Examen

- Make an online retreat with the *Ignatian Prayer Adventure*

- Participate in the conversation with the dotMagis blog and at **facebook.com/ignatianspirituality**